# Fodor's 95 Pocket New York City

Reprinted from *Fodor's New York City '95*

Fodor's Travel Publications, Inc.
New York • Toronto • London •
Sydney • Auckland

ISBN 0-679-02748-3

## Fodor's Pocket New York City

**Editors:** Christopher Billy and Anto Howard
**Contributors:** Robert Blake, Andrew Collins, Karen Cure, Janet Foley, Echo Garrett, Dick Kagan, Laura M. Kidder, David Low, Bevin McLaughlin, Paula Rackow, Mary Ellen Schultz, Kate Sekules, Jay Walman, Susan Spano Wells
**Creative Director:** Fabrizio La Rocca
**Cartographer:** David Lindroth
**Illustrator:** Karl Tanner
**Cover Photograph:** Paul Chesley/Photographers/Aspen
**Design:** Vignelli Associates

## Special Sales

Fodor's Travel Publications are available at special discounts for sales promotions or premiums. For more information, contact your local bookseller or write to Special Markets, Fodor's Travel Publications, 201 E. 50th Street, New York, NY 10022; Random House of Canada, Ltd., Marketing Dept., 1265 Aerowood Drive, Mississauga, Ontario L4W 1B9. Fodor's Travel Publications, 20 Vauxhall Bridge Road, London, England SW1V 2SA.

MANUFACTURED IN THE UNITED STATES OF AMERICA
10 9 8 7 6 5 4 3 2 1

# Contents

**Maps**

# Foreword

While every care has been taken to ensure the accuracy of the information in this guide, the passage of time will always bring change, and consequently, the publisher cannot accept responsibility for errors that may occur.

All prices and opening times quoted here are based on information supplied to us at press time. Hours and admission fees may change, however, and the prudent traveler will avoid inconvenience by calling ahead.

Fodor's wants to hear about your travel experiences, both pleasant and unpleasant. When a hotel or restaurant fails to live up to its billing, let us know and we will investigate the complaint and revise our entries where the facts warrant it.

Send your letters to the editors of Fodor's Travel Publications, 201 E. 50th Street, New York, NY 10022.

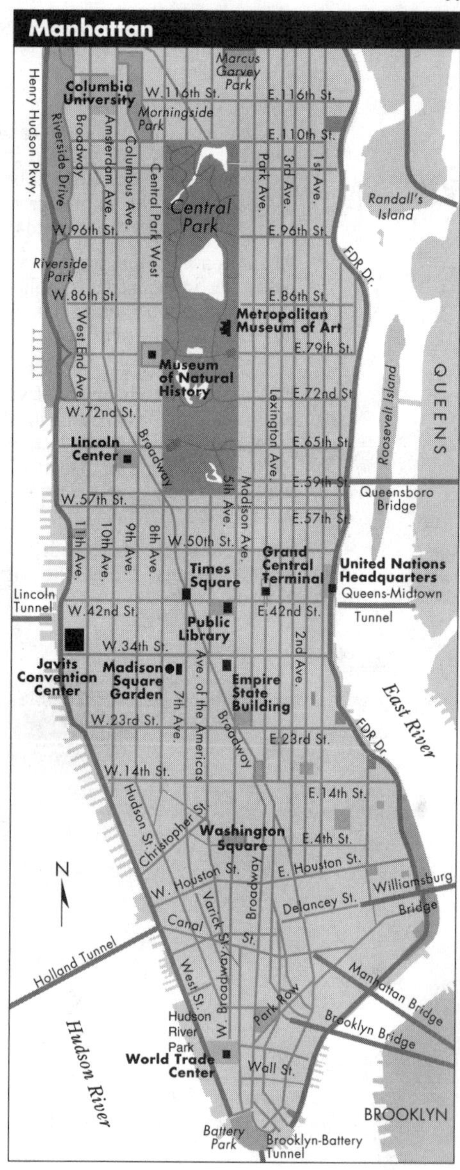
Manhattan
Marcus Garvey Park
Columbia University
W. 116th St.
E. 116th St.
Morningside Park
E. 110th St.
Henry Hudson Pkwy.
Riverside Drive
Broadway
Amsterdam Ave.
Columbus Ave.
Central Park West
Central Park
Park Ave.
3rd Ave.
1st Ave.
Randall's Island
W. 96th St.
E. 96th St.
FDR Dr.
Riverside Park
W. 86th St.
E. 86th St.
Metropolitan Museum of Art
West End Ave.
E. 79th St.
Museum of Natural History
E. 72nd St.
Lexington Ave.
Roosevelt Island
QUEENS
W. 72nd St.
Lincoln Center
Broadway
E. 65th St.
5th Ave.
Madison Ave.
E. 59th St.
Queensboro Bridge
W. 57th St.
E. 57th St.
11th Ave.
10th Ave.
9th Ave.
8th Ave.
W. 50th St.
Grand Central Terminal
United Nations Headquarters
Times Square
Queens-Midtown Tunnel
Lincoln Tunnel
W. 42nd St.
E. 42nd St.
Public Library
W. 34th St.
2nd Ave.
Javits Convention Center
Madison Square Garden
Empire State Building
East River
7th Ave.
Ave. of the Americas
Broadway
W. 23rd St.
E. 23rd St.
FDR Dr.
W. 14th St.
E. 14th St.
Hudson St.
Christopher St.
Washington Square
E. 4th St.
N
W. Houston St.
Broadway
E. Houston St.
Williamsburg Bridge
Delancey St.
Canal St.
Varick St.
Holland Tunnel
West St.
W. Broadway
Park Row
Manhattan Bridge
Brooklyn Bridge
Hudson River
Hudson River Park
World Trade Center
Wall St.
BROOKLYN
Battery Park
Brooklyn-Battery Tunnel

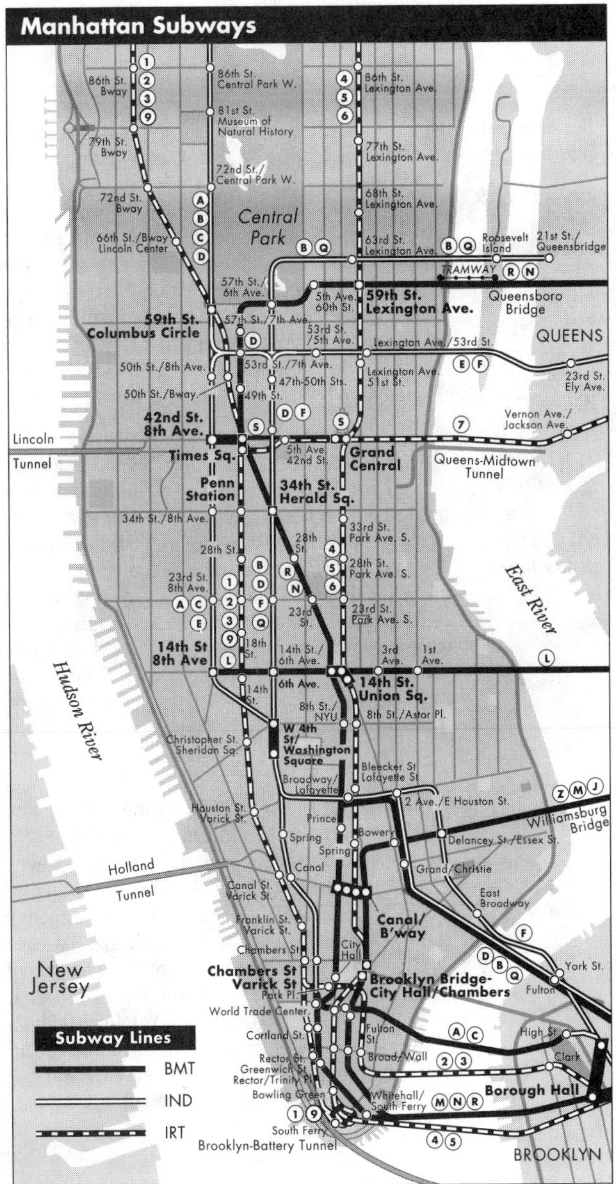
Manhattan Subways
Central Park
86th St. Bway
79th St. Bway
72nd St. Bway
66th St./Bway Lincoln Center
86th St. Central Park W.
81st St. Museum of Natural History
72nd St./Central Park W.
86th St. Lexington Ave.
77th St. Lexington Ave.
68th St. Lexington Ave.
63rd St. Lexington Ave.
Roosevelt Island
21st St./Queensbridge
TRAMWAY
57th St./6th Ave.
5th Ave. 60th St.
59th St. Lexington Ave.
Queensboro Bridge
QUEENS
59th St. Columbus Circle
57th St./7th Ave.
53rd St./5th Ave.
Lexington Ave./53rd St.
50th St./8th Ave.
53rd St./7th Ave.
47th-50th Sts.
Lexington Ave. 51st St.
23rd St. Ely Ave.
50th St./Bway
49th St.
Vernon Ave./Jackson Ave.
42nd St. 8th Ave.
Lincoln Tunnel
Times Sq.
5th Ave. 42nd St.
Grand Central
Queens-Midtown Tunnel
Penn Station
34th St. Herald Sq.
34th St./8th Ave.
33rd St. Park Ave. S.
28th St.
28th St.
28th St. Park Ave. S.
23rd St. 8th Ave.
23rd St.
23rd St. Park Ave. S.
East River
18th St.
14th St 8th Ave
14th St./6th Ave.
3rd Ave.
1st Ave.
Hudson River
6th Ave.
14th St.
14th St. Union Sq.
8th St./NYU
8th St./Astor Pl.
W 4th St/Washington Square
Christopher St. Sheridan Sq.
Bleecker St Lafayette St
Broadway/Lafayette
2 Ave./E Houston St.
Houston St. Varick St.
Prince
Williamsburg Bridge
Spring
Bowery
Spring
Delancey St./Essex St.
Holland Tunnel
Canal
Grand/Christie
Canal St. Varick St.
East Broadway
Canal/B'way
Franklin St. Varick St.
Chambers St
City Hall
York St.
New Jersey
Chambers St Varick St
Brooklyn Bridge-City Hall/Chambers
Fulton
Park Pl.
World Trade Center
Subway Lines
Cortland St.
Fulton St.
High St.
BMT
Rector St
Greenwich St
Rector/Trinity Pl
Broad/Wall
Clark
IND
Bowling Green
Whitehall/South Ferry
Borough Hall
IRT
South Ferry
Brooklyn-Battery Tunnel
BROOKLYN

# Introduction

*By Michael Adams*

*Senior writer for the business travel magazine* Successful Meetings, *Michael Adams finally moved to his hometown, New York City, 12 years ago.*

In 1925, the youthful songwriting team of Richard Rodgers and Larry Hart wrote "Manhattan," arguably the loveliest city anthem ever. "We'll have Manhattan, the Bronx, and Staten Island, too," it promises, drawing its images from the merry scramble that was the city more than 60 years ago: "sweet pushcarts," "baloney on a roll," a subway that "charms," Brighton Beach, Coney Island, and the popular comedy *Abie's Irish Rose*. "We'll turn Manhattan into an isle of joy," coos the refrain.

Several decades later, in 1989, an album called simply *New York*, by aging enfant terrible rocker Lou Reed, views the same city with glasses fogged by despair and cynicism: Drugs, crime, racism, and promiscuity reign in what Reed considers to be a sinkhole of "crudity, cruelty of thought and sound." His voice brittle with weary irony, he sings, "This is no time for celebration." Manhattan's "sweet pushcarts" now apparently overflow with deadly vials of crack.

So, whom to believe—Lou or Larry?

The truth of the matter is slippery, for New York has long been a mosaic of grand contradictions, a city for which there has never been—nor ever will be—a clear consensus. Hart himself took the city to task in another song, "Give It Back to the Indians," whose lyrics count off a litany of problems that still exist: crime, dirt, high prices, traffic jams, and all-around urban chaos. Yet for all that, millions live here, grumbling but happy, and millions more visit, curious as cats to find out what the magnificent fuss is all about.

I was in eighth grade in suburban Detroit when I first really became aware of New York. A friend's Manhattan-born mother still subscribed to the Sunday *New York Times*, and at their house I'd pore over the "Arts and Leisure" section, as rapt as an archaeologist with a cave painting. The details of what I read there have blurred, but I remember vividly the sensation I felt while reading: a combined anticipation and nostalgia so keen it bordered on pain. Although I had never been there, I was homesick for New York.

It's my home now, yet I can still understand and appreciate the impulse that draws visitors here.

And so whenever I get the New York blues, the best tonic for me is to glimpse the city through the eyes of a visitor. One day, after subway construction had rerouted me well out of my usual path, I found myself in the grimy Times Square station—hardly the place for a spiritual conversion. As usual I had that armor of body language that we New Yorkers reflexively assume to protect ourselves from strangers bent on (1) ripping us off, (2) doing us bodily harm, (3) converting us, (4) making sexual advances, or (5) being general pains-in-the-butt just for the hell of it. But that day, tucked away in a corner, was a group of musicians—not an uncommon sight in New York—playing the guitar, organ, and accordion with gusto and good spirits behind a homemade sign that dubbed them the "Argentinian Tango Company." Like many street musicians in Manhattan, they were *good*, but I was only half listening, too intent on cursing the city. Just as I passed the band, however, I noticed four teenagers drawn to the music—visitors surely, they were far too open and trusting to be anything else. Grinning as widely as the Argentinians, they began to perform a spontaneous imitation of flamenco dancing—clapping hands above their heads, raising their heels, laughing at themselves, and only slightly self-conscious. Passersby, myself included, broke into smiles. As I made my way to the subway platform, buoyed by the impromptu show, I once again forgave New York.

I wonder whether that was the moment one of those teenagers happened to fall in love with the city. It *can* happen in a single moment, to a visitor or to a longtime resident. Perhaps it hits during a stroll through Riverside Park after a blanketing snowfall, when trees have turned to crystal and the city feels a hush it knows at no other time; or when you turn a corner and spy, beyond a phalanx of RVs and a tangle of cables and high-beam lights, the filming of a new movie.

That moment could also come when the house lights begin to dim at the Metropolitan Opera, and the gaudily sparkling chandeliers make their magisterial ascent to the ceiling. You may even be smitten in that instant when, walking along the streets in the haze of a summer afternoon, you look up above the sea of anonymous faces to see—and be astonished by—the lofty rows of skyscrapers, splendid in their arrogance and power.

For some, of course, that special moment comes with a happy shock of recognition when they spot a street or building made familiar by movies or television, anything from *I Love Lucy* to *On the Waterfront*. At the Empire State Building, who can help but remember King Kong's pathetically courageous swing from its pinnacle? Or at the brooding Dakota, the chilling destiny created for Rosemary's baby within those fortresslike walls? And the miniature park on Sutton Place will always be where Woody Allen and Diane Keaton began their angst-ridden *Manhattan* love affair, with the 59th Street bridge gleaming beyond and Gershwin music swelling in the background.

There's a moment of sudden magic when a New York stereotype, seen so often on screen that it seems a joke, suddenly comes to life: when a gum-cracking waitress calls you "hon," or a stogie-sucking cabbie asks, "How 'bout them Yankees, Mac?" There's also the thrill of discovering one of New York's cities-within-the-city: Mulberry Street in Little Italy; Mott Street in Chinatown; Park Avenue's enclave of wealth and privilege; SoHo and TriBeCa, with their artistic types dressed in black from head to toe; or Sheridan Square, the nexus of the city's prominent lesbian and gay communities. The first glimpse of a landmark could begin the visitor's infatuation, too: frenetic Grand Central Station, abustle with suburban commuters; the concrete caverns of Wall Street, throbbing with power and ambition; or the Statue of Liberty, which neither cliché nor cheap souvenir can render common.

Excess and deprivation mingle here: As a limousine crawls lazily to take its pampered passengers to their luxe destination, it rolls past a threadbare beggar seeking the warmth that steams from the city's belly through an iron grate. It's a ludicrously bright cartoon and a sobering documentary, New York—almost too much for one city to be. It's maddening and it's thrilling; monstrous, yet beautiful beyond parallel.

And I envy anyone their first taste of it.

# 1 Essential Information

# Before You Go

## Tourist Information

The **New York Convention and Visitors Bureau** (2 Columbus Circle, New York, NY 10019, tel. 212/397–8222 or 212/484–1200, fax 212/484–1280) provides brochures, subway and bus maps, an up-to-date calendar of events, listings of hotels and weekend hotel packages, and discount coupons for Broadway shows. **The New York Division of Tourism** (1 Commerce Plaza, Albany, NY 12245, tel. 518/474–4116 or 800/225–5697) offers a free series of "I Love New York" booklets listing New York City attractions and tour packages.

## Tips for British Travelers

**Passports and Visas** British citizens need a valid 10-year passport. A visa is not necessary unless 1) you are planning to stay more than 90 days; 2) your trip is for purposes other than vacation; 3) you have at some time been refused a visa or refused admission to the United States, or have been required to leave by the U.S. Immigration and Naturalization Service; or 4) you do not have a return or onward ticket. You will need to fill out the Visa Waiver Form, 1–94W supplied by the airline. To apply for a visa or for more information, call the U.S. Embassy's Visa Information Line (tel. 0891/200–290; calls cost 48p per minute or 36p per minute cheap rate).

**Customs** British visitors age 21 or over may import the following into the United States: 200 cigarettes or 50 cigars or 2 kilograms of tobacco; one U.S. liter of alcohol; gifts to the value of $100. Restricted items include meat products, seeds, plants, and fruits. Never carry illegal drugs.

Returning to the United Kingdom, you may import duty-free 200 cigarettes, 100 cigarillos, 50 cigars or 250 grams of tobacco; 1 liter of spirits or 2 liters of fortified or sparkling wine; 2 liters of still table wine; 60 milliliters of perfume; 250 milliliters of toilet water; plus £36 worth of other goods, including gifts and souvenirs.

**Insurance** Most tour operators, travel agents, and insurance agents sell specialized policies covering accidents, medical expenses, personal liability, trip cancellation, and loss or theft of personal property. Some policies include coverage for delayed departure and legal expenses, winter-sports accidents, or motoring abroad. You can also purchase an annual travel-insurance policy valid for every trip you make during the year in which it's purchased (usually only trips of less than 90 days). Before you leave, make sure you will be covered if you have a preexisting medical condition or are pregnant; your insurers may not pay for routine or continuing treatment, or may require a note from your doctor certifying your fitness to travel.

The **Association of British Insurers,** a trade association representing 450 insurance companies, advises extra medical coverage for visitors to the United States.

For advice by phone or a free booklet, "Holiday Insurance," which sets out what to expect from a holiday-insurance policy and gives price guidelines, contact the Association of British Insurers (51 Gresham St., London EC2V 7HQ, tel. 0171/600–3333; 30 Gordon St., Glasgow G1 3PU, tel. 0141/226–3905; Scottish Provincial Bldg., Donegall Sq. W, Belfast BT1 6JE, tel. 01232/249176; call for other locations).

**Tour Operators** Tour operators offering packages to New York City include **Americana Vacations Ltd.** (Morley House, 320 Regent St., London W1R 5AD, tel. 0171/637–7853), **Jetsave** (Sussex House, London Rd., East Grinstead, Sussex RH19 1LD, tel. 01342/312033), **Key to America** (15 Feltham Rd., Ashford, Middx., TW15 1DQ, tel. 01784/248777), **Trailfinders** (42–50 Earls Court Rd., London W8 7RG, tel. 0171/937–5400; 58 Deansgate, Manchester M3 2FF, tel. 0161/839–3636), and **Transamerica Holidays** (3a Gatwick Metro Centre, Balcombe Rd., Horley RH6 9GA, tel. 01293/774441).

**Airfares** Fares vary enormously. Fares from consolidators are usually the cheapest, followed by promotional fares such as APEX (advance purchase excursion). A few phone calls should reveal the current picture. When comparing fares, don't forget to figure airport taxes and weekend supplements. Once you know which airline is going your way at the right time for the least money, book immediately, since seats at the lowest prices often sell out quickly. Travel agents will generally hold a reservation for up to 5 days, especially if you give a credit card number.

Seven airlines fly direct from Heathrow to La Guardia, JFK, or Newark: **British Airways** (tel. 0181/897–4000), **American Airlines** (tel. 01800/010151), **Virgin Atlantic** (tel. 01293/747747), **United Airlines** (tel. 01426/915500), **Air India** (0181/759-1818), **Kuwait Airways** (0181/745–7772), and **El Al** (0181/759–9771); BA and Virgin also serve Gatwick, as does **Continental Airlines** (tel. 01293/567977), and Virgin and AA both fly direct to Manchester, too. Flight time is approximately seven hours on all routes.

Some travel agencies that offer cheap fares to New York City include **Trailfinders** (*see above*), specialists in Round-The-World fares and independent travel: **Travel Cuts** (295a Regent St., London W1R 7YA, tel, 0171/637–3161), the Canadian Students' travel service; **Flightfile** (49 Tottenham Court Rd., London W1P 9RE, tel. 0171/700–2722), a flight-only agency.

**Travelers with Disabilities** Important information sources include the **Royal Association for Disability and Rehabilitation** (RADAR: 12 City Forum, 250 City Rd., London EC1V 8AF, tel. 0171/250–3222), which publishes travel information for people with disabilities in Britain, and **Mobility International** (228 Borough High St., London SE1 1JX, tel. 0171/403–5688), an international clearinghouse of travel information for people with disabilities.

## What to Pack

**Clothing** Jackets and ties are required for men in a number of restaurants. For sightseeing and casual dining, jeans and sneakers are acceptable just about anywhere in the city. Sneakers or other flat-heeled walking shoes are highly recommended for pounding the New York pavements.

**Miscellaneous** Bring an extra pair of eyeglasses or contact lenses in your carry-on luggage. If you have a health problem that requires a prescription drug, pack enough to last the duration of the trip.

**Luggage** *Regulations* Free airline baggage allowances depend on the airline, the route, and the class of your ticket; ask in advance. In general, on domestic flights you are entitled to check two bags—neither exceeding 62 inches, or 158 centimeters (length + width + height), or weighing more than 70 pounds (32 kilograms). A third piece may be brought aboard; its total dimensions are generally limited to less than 45 inches (114 centimeters), so it will fit easily under the seat in front of you or in the overhead compartment. In the United States the Federal Aviation Administration gives airlines broad latitude to limit carry-on allowances and tailor them to different aircraft and operational conditions. Charges for excess, oversize, or overweight pieces vary.

*Safeguarding Your Luggage* Before leaving home, itemize your bags' contents and their worth in case they go astray. To minimize that risk, tag them inside and out with your name, address, and phone number. (If you use your home address, cover it so that potential thieves can't see it.) Put a copy of your itinerary inside each bag, so that you can easily be tracked. At check-in, make sure that the tag attached by baggage handlers bears the correct three-letter code for your destination. If your bags do not arrive with you, or if you detect damage, immediately file a written report with the airline before you leave the airport.

*Insurance* In the event of loss, damage, or theft on domestic flights, airlines' liability is $1,250 per passenger, excluding the valuable items such as jewelry, cameras, and more that are listed in the fine print on your ticket. Excess-valuation insurance can be bought directly from the airline at check-in. Your homeowner's policy may fill the gap; or firms such as **The Travelers Companies** (1 Tower Sq., Hartford, CT 06183, tel. 203/277–0111 or 800/243–3174) and **Wallach and Company** (107 W. Federal St., Box 480, Middleburg, VA 22117, tel. 703/687–3166 or 800/237–6615) sell baggage insurance.

# Arriving and Departing

## From North America by Plane

Flights are either nonstop, direct, or connecting. A **nonstop** flight requires no change of plane and makes no stops. A **direct** flight stops at least once and can involve a change of plane, although the flight number remains the same; if the first leg is late, the second waits. This is not the case with a **connecting** flight, which involves a different plane and a different flight number.

**Airports and Airlines**

Virtually every major U.S. and foreign airline serves one or more of New York's three airports: **La Guardia Airport** (tel. 718/533–3400) and **JFK International Airport** (tel. 718/244–4444), both in the borough of Queens, and **Newark International Airport** (tel. 201/961–6000) in New Jersey.

U.S. carriers serving the New York area include **America West** (tel. 800/247–5692); **American** (tel. 800/433–7300); **Continental** (tel. 800/525–0280); **Delta** (tel. 800/221–1212); **Northwest** (tel. 800/225–2525); **TWA** (tel. 800/221–2000); **United** (tel. 800/241–6522); and **USAir** (tel. 800/428–4322).

**Between the Airports and Manhattan**

*La Guardia Airport*

**Taxis** cost $18–$23 plus tolls (which may be as high as $4) and take 20–40 minutes. Group taxi rides to Manhattan are available at taxi dispatch lines just outside the baggage-claim areas during most travel hours (except on Saturday and holidays). Group fares run $8–$9 per person (plus a share of tolls).

**Carey Airport Express buses** (tel. 718/632–0500, 800/456–1012, or 800/284–0909) depart for Manhattan every 20 minutes from 6 AM to midnight, from all terminals. It's a 20- to 30-minute ride to 42nd Street and Park Avenue, directly opposite Grand Central Terminal. The bus continues from there to the Port Authority Bus Terminal, the New York Hilton, Sheraton Manhattan, Holiday Inn Crowne Plaza, and Marriott Marquis hotels. Other midtown hotels are a short cab ride away. The bus fare is $8.50 ($10 to the hotels); pay the driver. **The Gray Line Air Shuttle Minibus** (tel. 212/315–3006 or 800/622–3427) serves major

Manhattan hotels directly to and from the airport. The fare is $12 per person; make arrangements at the airport's ground transportation center or use the courtesy phone.

*JFK International Airport*

**Taxis** cost $25–$30 plus tolls (which may be as much as $4) and take 35–60 minutes.

**Carey Airport Express buses** (tel. 718/632–0500, 800/456–1012, or 800/284–0909) depart for Manhattan every 30 minutes from 6 AM to midnight, from all JFK terminals. The ride to 42nd Street and Park Avenue (Grand Central Terminal) takes about one hour. The bus continues from there to the Port Authority Bus Terminal, the New York Hilton, Sheraton Manhattan, Holiday Inn Crowne Plaza, and Marriott Marquis hotels; it's a short cab ride to other midtown hotels. The bus fare is $11 ($12.50 to the hotels); pay the driver.

**The Gray Line Air Shuttle Minibus** (tel. 212/315–3006 or 800/622–3427) serves major Manhattan hotels directly from the airport; the cost is $15 per person. Make arrangements at the airport's ground transportation counter or use the courtesy phone.

*Newark Airport*

**Taxis** cost $28–$30 plus tolls ($4) and take 20–45 minutes. "Share and Save" group rates are available for up to four passengers between 8 AM and midnight; make arrangements with the airport's taxi dispatcher.

**NJ Transit Airport Express buses** (tel. 201/762–5100) depart every 15–30 minutes for the Port Authority Bus Terminal, at 8th Avenue and 42nd Street. From there it's a short cab ride to midtown hotels. The ride takes 30–45 minutes. The fare is $7; buy your ticket inside the airport terminal.

**Olympia Airport Express buses** (tel. 212/964–6233) leave for Grand Central Terminal, Penn Station, and 1 World Trade Center (next to the Vista hotel) about every 30 minutes from around 6 AM to midnight. The trip takes 35–45 minutes to Grand Central and Penn Station, 20 minutes to WTC. The fare is $7.

**The Gray Line Air Shuttle Minibus** (tel. 212/757–6840 or 800/622–3427) serves major Manhattan hotels directly to and from the airport. You pay

$17 per passenger; make arrangements at the airport's ground transportation center or use the courtesy phone.

## By Car

If you plan to drive into Manhattan, try to time your arrival in late morning or early afternoon. That way you'll avoid the morning and evening rush hours (a problem at the crossings into Manhattan) and lunch hour.

The **Lincoln Tunnel** (I–495), **Holland Tunnel,** and **George Washington Bridge** (I–95) connect Manhattan with the New Jersey Turnpike system and points west. The Lincoln Tunnel comes into midtown Manhattan; the Holland Tunnel into lower Manhattan; and the George Washington Bridge into northern Manhattan. Each of the three arteries requires a toll ($4 for cars) eastbound into New York, but no toll westbound.

From upstate New York, the city is accessible via the **New York (Dewey) Thruway** (I–87) (toll) to the **Major Deegan Expressway** (I–87) through the Bronx and across the **Triborough Bridge** ($2.50 toll), or via the **Taconic State Parkway** to the **Saw Mill River Parkway** ($1.25 toll bridge) into upper Manhattan.

From New England, the **Connecticut Turnpike** (I–95) connects with the **New England Thruway** (I–95) (toll) and then the **Bruckner Expressway** (I–278). Take the Bruckner to the **Triborough Bridge** ($2.50 toll) or to the **Cross Bronx Expressway,** which enters upper Manhattan on the west side ($1.25 toll bridge).

Manhattan has two major north–south arteries that run the length of the island. The **West Side Highway** skirts the Hudson River from Battery Park (where it's known as West Street) through midtown (it then becomes the Henry Hudson Parkway north of 72nd Street) and past the George Washington Bridge. Both the Holland and Lincoln tunnels enter Manhattan just a few blocks east of this route; the Cross Bronx Expressway connects with the Henry Hudson Parkway in northern Manhattan at the George Washington Bridge. **Franklin D. Roosevelt Drive**

(FDR Drive) runs along the East River from Battery Park into upper Manhattan, where it becomes Harlem River Drive north of 125th Street. Both the Queens Midtown Tunnel (East 36th Street) and the Queensboro Bridge (East 59th Street) can be entered a few blocks west of FDR Drive, which connects with the Triborough Bridge at East 125th Street.

Be forewarned: The deterioration of the bridges linking Manhattan, especially those spanning the East River, is a serious problem, and repairs will be ongoing for the next few years. Don't be surprised if a bridge is entirely or partially closed.

Driving within Manhattan can be a nightmare of gridlocked streets and predatory motorists. Free parking is difficult to find in midtown, and violators may be towed away literally within minutes. All over town, parking lots charge exorbitant rates—as much as $15 for two hours in some neighborhoods. If you do drive, don't plan to use your car much for traveling within Manhattan.

## Car Rentals

If you find you absolutely need a car—perhaps for a weekend escape or because Manhattan is part of a longer trip—you'll have to sort out Manhattan's confusing array of car-rental possibilities. Although rates were once cheaper out of Newark airport, that is no longer the case; prices charged by national firms are the same at Newark, JFK, and La Guardia, as well as at Manhattan rental locations. Companies with multiple Manhattan and airport locations include **Avis** (tel. 800/331–1212, 800/879–2847 in Canada); **Budget** (tel. 800/527–0700); **Dollar** (tel. 800/800–4000); **Hertz** (tel. 800/654–3131, 800/263–0600 in Canada); and **National** (tel. 800/227–7368). Some regional budget companies, such as **Rent-A-Wreck** (tel. 212/721–0080), offer lower rates. If you are flying into La Guardia or JFK, you might look into some local Queens agencies with lower rates, such as **Universal** (tel. 718/786–0786). **Sunshine Rent-A-Car** (tel. 212/989–7260) is good for budget rentals in Greenwich Village. Unlimited-mileage rates range from $64 per day for an economy car to $82 for a large car; weekly unlimited-mileage rates range from $226 to $330. This does not include tax, which in New York State is 12¼% on car rentals.

**Extra Charges** Picking up the car in one city and leaving it in another may entail substantial drop-off charges or one-way service fees. Some rental agencies will charge you extra if you return the car *before* the time specified on your contract. Ask before making unscheduled drop-offs. Fill the tank when you turn in the vehicle to avoid being charged for refueling at what you'll swear is the most expensive pump in town.

**Insurance and Collision Damage Waiver** In general if you have an accident, you are responsible for the automobile. Car rental companies may offer a collision damage waiver (CDW), which ranges in cost from $4 to $14 a day. You should decline the CDW only if you are certain you are covered through your personal insurer or credit card company. California, New York, and Illinois have outlawed the sale of CDW altogether.

## By Train

**Amtrak** (tel. 800/872–7245) offers frequent service within the Northeast Corridor, between Boston and Washington, DC. Trains arrive at and depart from **Pennsylvania Station** (31st–33rd Sts., between 7th and 8th Aves.). Amtrak trains serve Penn Station from upstate New York, Montréal, the Southeast, Midwest, and Far West. Penn Station also handles **Long Island Railroad** trains (tel. 718/217–5477), with service to and from all over Long Island, and **New Jersey Transit** trains (tel. 201/762–5100), with frequent service from the northern and central regions of New Jersey.

**Metro-North Commuter Railroad** (tel. 212/340–3000) serves the northern suburbs and Connecticut as far east as New Haven from Grand Central Terminal. The other Metro-North Manhattan stop is at 125th Street and Park Avenue in East Harlem—not a good place to get off the train unless you are visiting this neighborhood.

**PATH Trains** (tel. 201/963–2557, 212/466–7649, or 800/234–7284) run 24 hours a day to New York

City from terminals in Hoboken, Jersey City, Harrison, and Newark, New Jersey; they connect with seven major New Jersey Transit commuter lines at Hoboken Station, Broad Street Station (Newark), and Penn Station (Newark). PATH trains stop in Manhattan at the World Trade Center and along 6th Avenue at Christopher Street, 9th Street, 14th Street, 23rd Street, and 33rd Street. They run every 10 minutes on weekdays, every 15–30 minutes on weeknights, and every 20–30 minutes on weekends. The fare is $1.

## By Bus

All long-haul and commuter bus lines feed into the **Port Authority Terminal** (tel. 212/564–8484), a mammoth multilevel structure that occupies a nearly 2-square-block area between 40th and 42nd streets and 8th and 9th avenues. Though it was recently modernized and is fairly clean, large numbers of vagrants make the terminal an uncomfortable place to spend much time. Especially with night arrivals, plan to move through the terminal swiftly. Beware of hustlers trying to help you hail a cab on 8th Avenue—they will demand a tip for performing this unnecessary service and can be hostile and aggressive if crossed.

For information on any service into or out of the Port Authority Terminal, call 212/564–8484. Some of the individual bus lines serving New York include **Greyhound** (tel. 800/231–2222); **Adirondack Pine Hill Trailways** from upstate New York (tel. 800/225–6815); **Bonanza Bus Lines** from New England (tel. 800/556–3815); **Martz Trailways** from northeastern Pennsylvania (tel. 800/233–8604); **New Jersey Transit** from around New Jersey (tel. 201/762–5100); **Peter Pan Bus Lines** from New England (tel. 413/781–2900); and **Vermont Transit** from New England (tel. 802/862–9671).

# Staying in New York

## Important Addresses and Numbers

**Tourist Information** **New York Convention and Visitors Bureau.** The main office is at 2 Columbus Circle (tel. 212/397-8222) and is open weekdays 9–6, weekends 10–6.

**Emergencies** Dial 911 for **police, fire,** or **ambulance** in an emergency.

**Deaf Emergency Teletypewriter** (tel. 800/342-4357), for medical, fire, and ambulance emergencies.

*Doctor* **Doctors On Call, 24-hour house-call service** (tel. 212/737-2333). Near midtown, 24-hour emergency rooms are open at **St. Luke's-Roosevelt Hospital** (58th St. at 9th Ave., tel. 212/523-6800) and **St. Vincent's Hospital** (7th Ave. and 11th St., tel. 212/790-7997).

*Dentist* The **Dental Emergency Service** (tel. 212/679-3966; after 8 PM, tel. 212/679-4172) will make a referral.

*24-Hour Pharmacy* **Kaufman's Pharmacy** (Lexington Ave. and 50th St., tel. 212/755-2266) is convenient but its prices are exorbitant; **Genovese** (2nd Ave. at 67th St., tel. 212/772-0104) is less expensive. Before 10 or 11 PM, look for a pharmacy in a neighborhood that keeps late hours, such as Greenwich Village or the Upper West Side for better deals.

## Getting Around

**By Subway** The 230-mile subway system operates 24 hours a day and, especially within Manhattan, serves most of the places you'll want to visit. It's cheaper than a cab and, during the workweek, often faster than either cabs or buses. The trains have finally been rid of their graffiti (some New Yorkers, of course, perversely miss the colorful old trains), and sleek new air-conditioned cars predominate on many lines. The New York subway deserves much of its negative image, however. Many trains are crowded, dirty, and noisy, and even occasionally unsafe. Although trains are scheduled to run frequently, especially during rush hours, you never know when some incident somewhere on the line may stall traffic indefinitely. Unsavory characters lurk around certain stations, and panhandlers frequently work their way through the cars. Don't write off the subway—some 3.5 million passengers ride it every day without incident—but stay alert at all times.

The subway fare at press time was $1.25, but transit authority officials were already predicting that it would be raised to $1.50, which may have occurred by the time you visit New York. Reduced fares are available for handicapped people and senior citizens during nonrush hours. If you're just taking a few trips, you should pay with tokens; they are sold at token booths that are *usually* open at each station. It is advisable to buy several tokens at one time to prevent waiting in line later. For four or more subway trips, you might find it easier to use the MTA's new MetroCard, a thin, plastic card with a magnetic strip that you swipe through a reader. The cards were introduced in early 1994, and subway stations are gradually upgrading to be able to accept them. By 1995, most major subway stations will accept the cards. They are sold at all subway stations where they are accepted; at some Metro-North and Long Island Rail Road commuter rail stations; and at some stores—look for an "Authorized Sales Agent" sign. You can buy a card for a minimum of $5 (4 trips) and a maximum of $80, in $5 increments. You can add more money to a card, and more than one person can use the same card: Swipe it through once for each rider. Both tokens and MetroCards permit unlimited transfers within the system.

This book's subway map covers the most-visited parts of Manhattan. Maps of the full subway system are posted on many trains and at some stations, but don't rely on finding one when you need it. You may be able to pick up free maps at token booths, too, but they are often out of stock. Make sure the map you refer to is up-to-date—lengthy repair programs can cause reroutings that last long enough for new "temporary" maps to be printed.

**By Bus** Most buses follow easy-to-understand routes along the Manhattan grid. Routes go up or down the north–south avenues, or east and west on the major two-way crosstown streets. Most bus routes operate 24 hours, but service is infrequent late at night. Buses are great for sightseeing, but traffic jams—a potential threat at any time or place in Manhattan—can make rides maddeningly slow. Certain bus routes now offer "Limited-Stop Service"; buses on these routes stop only at major cross streets and transfer points and can save traveling time. The "Limited-Stop" buses usually run on weekdays and during rush hours. For information about routes, bus stops, and hours of operation, call 718/330–1234 daily 6–9.

Bus fare is the same as subway fare: $1.25 at press time, in coins (no pennies; no change is given) or a subway token or MetroCard (some buses will start accepting the card in 1995, and all will accept them by the end of 1996, according to the MTA). When you get on the bus you can ask the driver for a free transfer coupon, good for one change to an intersecting route. Legal transfer points are listed on the back of the slip. Transfers have time limits of at least two hours, often longer. You cannot use the transfer to enter the subway system.

Guide-A-Rides, which consist of route maps and schedules, are posted at many bus stops in Manhattan and at major stops throughout the other boroughs. Each of the five boroughs of New York has a separate bus map, and they are scarcer than hens' teeth. They are occasionally available in subway token booths, but never on buses. The best places to obtain them are the Convention and Visitors Bureau at Columbus Circle or the information kiosks in Grand Central Terminal and Penn Station.

**By Taxi** Taxis are usually easy to hail on the street or from a taxi rank in front of major hotels. You can tell if a cab is available by checking its rooftop light; if the center panel is lit, the driver is ready to take passengers. Taxis cost $1.50 for the first ⅕ mile, 25¢ for each ⅕ mile thereafter, and 25¢ for each 75 seconds not in motion. A 50¢ surcharge is added to rides begun between 8 PM and 6 AM. There is no charge for extra passengers, but you must pay any bridge or tunnel tolls incurred during your trip (sometimes a driver will personally pay a toll to keep moving quickly, but that amount will be added to the fare when the ride is over). Taxi drivers also expect a 15% tip. Barring performance above and beyond the call of duty, don't feel obliged to give them more.

## Guided Tours

**Orientation Tours**

*Boat Tours*

The most pleasant way to get a crash orientation to Manhattan is aboard a **Circle Line Cruise.** Once you've finished the three-hour, 35-mile circumnavigation of Manhattan, you'll have a good idea of where things are and what you want to see next. Narrations are as interesting and individualized as the guides who deliver them. *Pier 83, west end of 42nd St., tel. 212/563–3200. Fare: $16 adults, $8 children under 12. Operates early Mar.–Dec., daily.*

For a shorter excursion, the **TNT Express,** a hydroliner, will show you the island of Manhattan in 75 minutes. *Pier 11, 2 blocks south of South St. Seaport, tel. 800/342–5868. Fare: $15 adults, $13 senior citizens, $8 children under 12, children under 5 free. Boats depart Apr.–Sept., weekdays and Sat. at noon and 2 PM.*

**World Yacht Cruises** (Pier 81, W. 42nd St. at Hudson River, tel. 212/630–8100) serve lunch ($27.50) and Sunday brunch ($39.95) on two-hour cruises, and dinner (Sun.–Thurs. $62; Fri.–Sat. $69.50; drinks extra) on three-hour cruises. The Continental cuisine is restaurant quality, and there's even music and dancing on board. The cruises run daily year-round, weather permitting.

***The Spirit of New York*** (Pier 9, three blocks south of South Street Seaport on East River, tel. 212/742–7278) sails on lunch ($22.95), brunch ($29.95), dinner ($42.95–$48.95), and moonlight cocktail ($18) cruises.

At South Street Seaport's Pier 16 you can take two- or three-hour voyages to New York's past aboard the iron cargo schooner ***Pioneer*** (tel. 212/669–9400) or 90-minute tours of New York Harbor aboard the sidewheeler ***Andrew Fletcher*** or the ***DeWitt Clinton,*** a re-created steamboat (tel. 212/269–3200).

*Bus Tours* **Gray Line** (254 W. 54th St., tel. 212/397–2620) offers a taste of yesteryear with their "NY Trolley Tour" on coaches replicating New York trolleys of the '30s. **Central Park Trolley Tours** tempts visitors to explore parts of the park that even native New Yorkers may have never seen. Or climb to the top of an authentic London double-deck bus operated by **New York Doubledecker Tours** (tel. 212/967–6008); hop on and off to visit attractions as often as you like.

*Helicopter Tours* **Island Helicopter** (heliport at E. 34th St. and East River, tel. 212/683–4575) offers four fly-over options, from $47 (for 7 miles) to $119 (for 35 miles). From the West Side, **Liberty Helicopter Tours** (heliport at W. 30th St. and Hudson River, tel. 212/465–8905) has three tours ranging from $55 to $119.

**Special-Interest Tours** **Backstage on Broadway** (tel. 212/575–8065) is a talk about the Broadway theater held in an actual theater, given by a theater professional. Reservations are mandatory; groups of 25 or more only. Call **The Metropolitan Opera House Backstage** (tel. 212/769–7020) for a tour of the scene and costume shops, stage area, and rehearsal facilities. **Stardom Tours** (tel. 800/STARDOM) offers a tour around the city emphasizing celebrity homes and memorable movie locations. **Gallery Passports** (tel. 212/288–3578) takes you to galleries and museums in Manhattan. **Literary Tours of Greenwich Village** (tel. 212/924–0239) walks in the footsteps of famous American writers. **Harlem Your Way!** (tel. 212/690–1687), **Harlem Spirituals, Inc.** (tel. 212/757–0425), and **Penny Sightseeing Co., Inc.** (tel. 212/410–0080) offer bus and walking tours and Sunday gospel trips to Harlem. **The Lower East Side Tenement Museum** (tel. 212/431–0233) offers Sunday tours through former immigrant communities. **River to River Downtown Tours** (tel. 212/321–2823) specializes in lower Manhattan for two-hour walking tours.

**Walking Tours** **New York City Cultural Walking Tours** (tel. 212/979–2388) focuses on the city's architecture, landmarks, memorials, outdoor art, and historic sites. **Sidewalks of New York** (tel. 212/517–0201 or 212/662–6300) hits the streets from various thematic angles—"Ye Old Tavern" tours,

"Celebrity Home" tours, "Famous Murder Sites," "Chelsea Saints and Sinners," and so forth. These walks are offered on weekends year-round; weekday tours are available by appointment. **Adventure on a Shoestring** (tel. 212/265–2663) is an organization dating from 1963 that explores New York neighborhoods. Tours are scheduled periodically for $5 per person. **Big Onion Walking Tours** (tel. 212/439–1090) has theme tours: try "From Naples to Bialystock to Beijing: A Multi-Ethnic Eating Tour." **Citywalks** (tel. 212/989–2456) offers two-hour walking tours exploring various neighborhoods in depth, weekends at 1 PM for $12. The **Municipal Art Society** (tel. 212/935–3960) operates a series of bus and walking tours. The **Museum of the City of New York** (tel. 212/534–1672) sponsors Sunday afternoon walking tours. **SoHo Art Tours** (tel. 212/431–8005) gives an inside look at the SoHo art community with visits to galleries, artists' studios, and the area's unusual cast-iron buildings. The **Urban Park Rangers** (tel. 212/427–4040) offer weekend walks and workshops, most of them free, in city parks.

The most comprehensive listing of tours offered during a particular week is published in the "Other Events" section of *New York* magazine's "Cue" listings.

**Self-Guided Walking Tours**

The **New York Convention and Visitors Bureau's** "I Love New York Visitors Guide and Map" is available at the bureau's information center (2 Columbus Circle, tel. 212/397–8222). Walkers in Brooklyn can pick up two maps—"Brooklyn on Tour" and "Downtown Brooklyn Walking Tours"—as well as a handy "Brooklyn Neighborhood Book," all free of charge, at the public affairs desk of the **Brooklyn Borough President**'s office (209 Joralemon St., 3rd Floor).

# 2 Exploring Manhattan

### Orientation

Above 14th Street the streets form a regular grid pattern, imposed in 1811. Consecutively numbered streets run east and west (crosstown), while broad avenues, most of them also numbered, run north (uptown) or south (downtown). The chief exceptions are Broadway (which runs on a diagonal from East 14th to West 79th streets) and the thoroughfares that hug the shores of the Hudson and East rivers.

Fifth Avenue is the east–west dividing line for street addresses: in both directions, they increase in regular increments from there. An address at 552 3rd Avenue, for example, will not necessarily be anywhere near 552 2nd Avenue. New Yorkers themselves cannot master the complexities of this system, so in their daily dealings they usually include cross-street references along with avenue addresses (as far as possible, we follow that custom in this book). New Yorkers also rely on the handy Manhattan Address Locator found in the front of the local phone book.

Below 14th Street—the area that was already settled before the 1811 grid was decreed—Manhattan streets are disordered. They may be aligned with the shoreline or they may twist along the route of an ancient cow path. There's an East Broadway and a West Broadway, both of which run north–south and neither of which is an extension of plain old Broadway. Logic won't help you below 14th Street; only a good street map and good directions will.

# Exploring

### Tour 1: Rockefeller Center

*Numbers in the margin correspond to points of interest on the Midtown map.*

Begun during the Great Depression of the 1930s by John D. Rockefeller, this 19-building complex occupies nearly 22 acres of prime real estate between 5th and 7th avenues and 47th and 52nd streets. Its central cluster of buildings are smooth shafts of warm-hued limestone, stream-

Manhattan Neighborhoods
HARLEM
Marcus Garvey Park
Randall's Island
Morningside Park
W. 116th St.
E. 116th St.
E. 110th St.
Henry Hudson Pkwy.
Riverside Drive
Broadway
Amsterdam Ave.
Columbus Ave.
Central Park West
Central Park
Ward's Island
W. 96th St.
E. 96th St.
UPPER WEST SIDE
UPPER EAST SIDE
W. 86th St.
E. 86th St.
West End Ave.
E. 79th St.
Park Ave.
W. 72nd St.
E. 72nd St.
QUEENS
Roosevelt Island
FDR Dr.
Broadway
E. 65th St.
E. 59th St.
Queensboro Bridge
W. 57th St.
E. 57th St.
5th Ave.
11th Ave.
10th Ave.
9th Ave.
8th Ave.
3rd Ave.
1st Ave.
Queens-Midtown Tunnel
W. 42nd St.
E. 42nd St.
Lincoln Tunnel
MIDTOWN
Ave. of the Americas
Madison Ave.
Lexington Ave.
2nd Ave.
W. 34th St.
7th Ave.
East River
W. 23rd St.
Broadway
E. 23rd St.
CHELSEA
GRAMERCY
W. 14th St.
E. 14th St.
Hudson River
GREENWICH VILLAGE
EAST VILLAGE
West St.
E. Houston St.
W. Houston St.
Williamsburg Bridge
SOHO
LITTLE ITALY
Broadway
Canal St.
Holland Tunnel
CHINA-TOWN
TRIBECA
W. Broadway
Manhattan Bridge
Chambers St.
Brooklyn Bridge
N
LOWER MANHATTAN
BROOKLYN
Battery Park
Brooklyn-Battery Tunnel

lined with glistening aluminum, but the real genius of the complex's design was its intelligent use of public space: plazas, concourses, and street-level shops that create a sense of community for the nearly quarter of a million human beings who use it daily.

Let's begin the tour with a proud symbol of the center's might: the huge statue of Atlas supporting the world that stands sentry before the
1 **International Building** (5th Ave., between 50th and 51st Sts.). The building, with a lobby inspired by ancient Greece and fitted with Grecian marble, houses many foreign consulates, international airlines, and a U.S. passport office.

One block south on 5th Avenue, between 49th and 50th streets, you'll come to the head of the **Channel Gardens,** a promenade with six pools surrounded by flowerbeds filled with seasonal plantings, conceived by artists, floral designers, and sculptors—10 shows a season. They are called the Channel Gardens because they separate the British building to the north from the French building to the south (above each building's entrance is a coat of arms bearing that country's national symbols). The French building contains among other shops the **Librairie de France,** which sells French-language books, periodicals, and records; its surprisingly large basement contains a Spanish bookstore and a foreign-dictionary store.

At the foot of the Channel Gardens is perhaps the most famous sight in Rockefeller Center (if not all of New York): the great gold-leaf statue of the fire-stealing Greek hero **Prometheus,**
2 sprawled on his ledge above the **Lower Plaza.** A quotation from Aeschylus is carved into the red granite wall behind, and 50 jets of water spray around the statue. The plaza's trademark ice-skating rink is open from October through April; the rest of the year, it becomes an open-air café. In December the plaza is decorated with an enormous live Christmas tree. On the Esplanade above the Lower Plaza, flags of the United Nations' members alternate with flags of the states.

American Craft Museum, **7**
Chrysler Building, **12**
Ford Foundation Building, **13**
GE Building, **3**
Grand Central Terminal, **11**
International Building, **1**
Lower Plaza, **2**
Museum of Modern Art, **6**
Museum of Television and Radio, **5**
New York Public Library, **10**
Radio City Music Hall, **4**
St. Patrick's Cathedral, **8**
Times Square, **9**
United Nations Headquarters, **14**

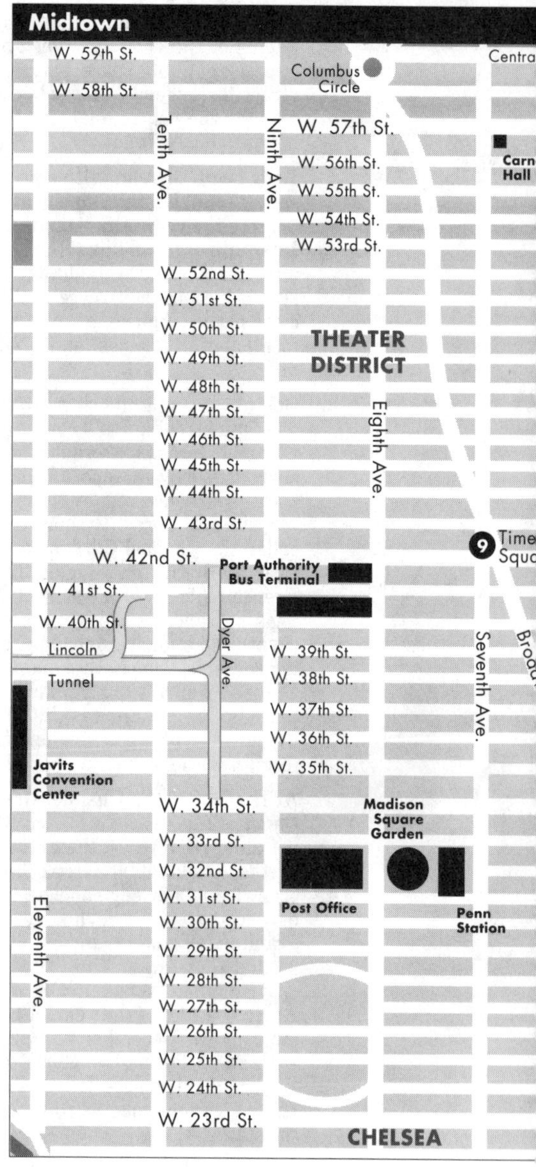

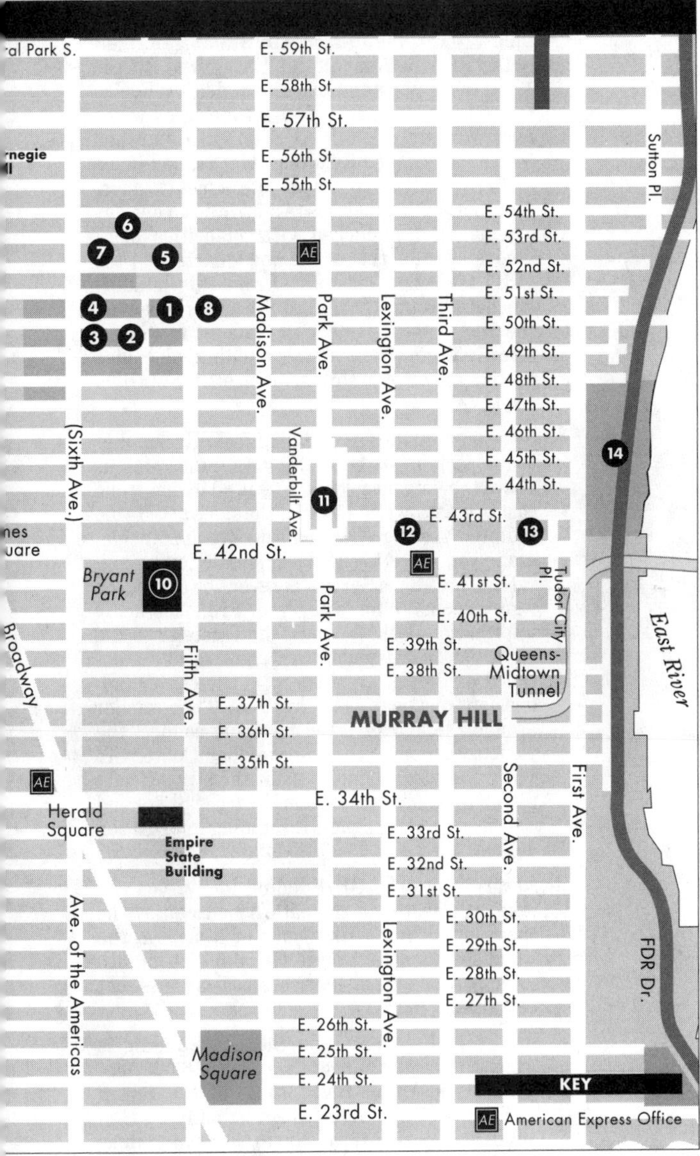

ral Park S.
E. 59th St.
E. 58th St.
E. 57th St.
E. 56th St.
E. 55th St.
E. 54th St.
E. 53rd St.
E. 52nd St.
E. 51st St.
E. 50th St.
E. 49th St.
E. 48th St.
E. 47th St.
E. 46th St.
E. 45th St.
E. 44th St.
E. 43rd St.
E. 42nd St.
E. 41st St.
E. 40th St.
E. 39th St.
E. 38th St.
E. 37th St.
E. 36th St.
E. 35th St.
E. 34th St.
E. 33rd St.
E. 32nd St.
E. 31st St.
E. 30th St.
E. 29th St.
E. 28th St.
E. 27th St.
E. 26th St.
E. 25th St.
E. 24th St.
E. 23rd St.
rnegie
ll
Sutton Pl.
Madison Ave.
Park Ave.
Lexington Ave.
Third Ave.
Vanderbilt Ave.
(Sixth Ave.)
nes
uare
Bryant Park
Broadway
Fifth Ave.
Tudor City Pl.
Queens-Midtown Tunnel
East River
MURRAY HILL
Herald Square
Empire State Building
Second Ave.
First Ave.
FDR Dr.
Ave. of the Americas
Madison Square
KEY
AE American Express Office

The backdrop to the Lower Plaza is the center's
3 tallest tower, the 70-story **GE Building** (formerly the RCA Building until GE acquired RCA in 1986), occupying the block bounded by Rockefeller Plaza, Avenue of the Americas (which New Yorkers call 6th Avenue), and 49th and 50th streets. The block-long street called Rockefeller Plaza, officially a private street (to maintain that status, it closes to all traffic on one day a year), is often choked with celebrities' black limousines, for this is the headquarters of the NBC television network. From this building emanated some of the first TV programs ever; the *Today* show has been broadcast from here since 1952, and a shot of this building is included in the opening credit sequence of *Saturday Night Live*.

As you enter the GE Building from Rockefeller Plaza, look up at the striking sculpture of Zeus above the entrance doors, executed in limestone cast in glass by Lee Lawrie, the same artist who sculpted the big Atlas on 5th Avenue. Inside, crane your neck to see the dramatic ceiling mural by Jose Maria Sert: Wherever you stand, the figure seems to be facing you. From the lobby information desk, go down the escalator in the right-hand corner and turn right to find a detailed exhibit on the history of the center (admission free; open weekdays 9–5). Then wander around the marble catacombs that connect the various components of Rockefeller Center. To find your way around, consult the strategically placed directories or obtain the free "Shops and Services Guide" at the GE Building information desk.

Returning to the GE Building lobby, you can take an elevator to the 65th floor to enjoy the spectacular view with drinks or a meal at the **Rainbow Room.** Exit the GE Building on 6th Avenue to see the allegorical mosaics above that entrance.

Across 50th Street from the GE Building is America's largest indoor theater, the 6,000-seat
4 **Radio City Music Hall.** Home of the fabled Rockettes chorus line (which actually started out in St. Louis in 1925), Radio City was built as a movie theater with a stage suitable for live

shows as well. Its days as a first-run movie house are long over, but after an announced closing in 1978 Radio City has had an amazing comeback, producing concerts, awards presentations, and special events, along with its own Christmas and Easter extravaganzas. On most days you can take a one-hour tour of the premises. *Tel. 212/247–4777; tour information, 212/632–4041. Tour admission: $9 adults, $5 children under 6. Tours usually leave from main lobby every 30 min, Mon.–Sat. 10–4:45, Sun. 11:15–4:45.*

Later additions to Rockefeller Center include 6th Avenue's skyscraper triplets—the first between 47th and 48th streets, the second (the **McGraw-Hill Building**) between 48th and 49th streets, and the third between 49th and 50th streets—and their cousin immediately to the north, the **Time & Life Building,** between 50th and 51st streets. All have street-level plazas, but the most interesting is McGraw-Hill's, where a 50-foot steel sun triangle points to the seasonal positions of the sun at noon and a pool demonstrates the relative size of the planets.

NBC isn't the only network headquartered in Manhattan. The **CBS Building** is a black monolith popularly called Black Rock, on 6th Avenue between 52nd and 53rd streets. (ABC, once a close neighbor, has now moved its main office to 66th Street on the West Side.) From here, you can choose among a cluster of museums: the Museum of Television and Radio, the American Craft Museum, or the major collection at the Museum of Modern Art. Go east on 52nd Street 5 to the **Museum of Television and Radio,** housed in a new limestone building by Philip Johnson and John Burgee that reminds everyone of a 1930s-vintage radio. Three galleries exhibit photographs and artifacts relating to the history of broadcasting, but most visitors to this museum come to sit at a console and sample its stupendous collection of more than 32,000 TV shows, 13,000 commercials, and 16,000 radio programs. *25 W. 52nd St., tel. 212/621–6800 for daily events or 212/621–6600 for other information. Suggested contribution: $5 adults, $4 students, $3 senior citizens and under 13. Open*

*Tues.–Wed. and Fri.–Sun. noon–6, Thurs. noon–8.*

Just east of the Museum of Television and Radio, you'll pass the famous restaurant **The "21" Club,** with its trademark row of jockey statuettes parading along the wrought-iron balcony. Now wonderfully restored after an extensive renovation, it still has a burnished men's-club atmosphere and a great downstairs bar. In the movie *The Sweet Smell of Success,* Burt Lancaster as a powerful Broadway columnist held court at his regular table here, besieged by Tony Curtis as a pushy young publicist.

To reach the other museums, on 53rd Street, walk toward 5th Avenue and turn left to cut through the shopping arcade of 666 5th Avenue.
6 On the north side of 53rd is the **Museum of Modern Art** (MOMA), in a bright and airy six-story structure built around a secluded sculpture garden. In the second- and third-floor galleries of painting and sculpture, some of the world's most famous modern paintings are displayed: Van Gogh's *Starry Night,* Picasso's *Les Demoiselles d'Avignon,* Matisse's *Dance.* The collection also includes photography, architecture, decorative arts, drawings, prints, illustrated books, and films. Afternoon and evening film shows, mostly foreign films and classics, are free with the price of admission; tickets are distributed in the lobby on the day of the performance, and often they go fast. Programs change daily; call 212/708–9480 for a schedule. There's a good bookstore just off the lobby, and the even more interesting MOMA Design Store across the street. And leave time to sit outside in that wonderful Sculpture Garden. *11 W. 53rd St., tel. 212/708–9500. Admission: $7.50 adults, $4.50 students and senior citizens; children under 16 free. Pay what you wish Thurs. and Fri. 5–8:30. Open Sat.–Tues. 11–6, Thurs. and Fri. 11–8:30.*

7 On the south side of 53rd, the **American Craft Museum** spotlights the work of contemporary American and international craftspersons working in clay, glass, fabric, wood, metal, paper, or even chocolate. Distinctions between "craft" and "high art" become irrelevant here, for much of this work is provocative and fun to look at. *40*

*W. 53rd St., tel. 212/956–3535. Admission: $4.50 adults, $2 students and senior citizens. Open Tues. 10–8, Wed.–Sun. 10–5.*

Back on 5th Avenue, at 51st street, is Gothic-
8 style **St. Patrick's,** the Roman Catholic Cathedral of New York. Dedicated to the patron saint of the Irish—then and now one of New York's principal ethnic groups—the white marble and stone structure was begun in 1858, consecrated in 1879, and completed in 1906. Among the statues in the alcoves around the nave is a striking modern interpretation of the first American-born saint, Mother Elizabeth Seton. From outside, catch one of the city's most photographed views: the ornate white spires of St. Pat's against the black glass curtain of **Olympic Tower,** a multiuse building of shops, offices, and luxury apartments.

## Tour 2: Across 42nd Street

While it may not exactly be the Crossroads of
9 the World, as it is often called, **Times Square** is one of New York's principal energy centers. It's one of many New York City "squares" that are actually triangles formed by the angle of Broadway slashing across a major avenue—in this case, crossing 7th Avenue at 42nd Street. The square itself is occupied by the former Times Tower, now resheathed in white marble and called **One Times Square Plaza.** When the *New York Times* moved into its new headquarters on December 31, 1904, it publicized the event with a fireworks show at midnight, thus starting a New Year's Eve tradition. Each December 31, workmen on this roof lower a 200-pound ball down the flagpole by hand, just as they have since 1908. The huge intersection below is mobbed with revelers, and when the ball hits bottom on the stroke of midnight, pandemonium ensues.

The present headquarters of the *New York Times* (229 W. 43rd St.) occupies much of the block between 7th and 8th avenues; look for the blue delivery vans lined up along 43rd Street. From 44th to 51st streets, the cross streets west of Broadway are lined with some 30 major theaters (*see* Chapter 6). This has been the city's main theater district since the turn of the century; movie theaters joined the fray beginning in the 1920s. As the theaters drew crowds of people in the evenings, advertisers began to mount huge electric signs here, which gave the intersection its distinctive nighttime glitter.

Between 40th and 42nd streets on 5th Avenue, you'll find the central research building of the
10 **New York Public Library.** This 1911 masterpiece of Beaux Arts design was financed largely by John Jacob Astor. Its grand front steps are guarded by two crouching marble lions—dubbed "Patience" and "Fortitude" by Mayor Fiorello La Guardia, who said he visited the facility to "read between the lions." After admiring the white marble neoclassical facade (crammed with statues, as is typical of Beaux Arts buildings), walk through the bronze front doors into the grand marble lobby with its sweeping double staircase. Turn left and peek into the Periodicals Room, decorated with trompe l'oeil paintings by Richard Haas commemorating New York's importance as a publishing center. Then take a (quiet) look upstairs at the huge, high-ceilinged main reading room, a haven of scholarly calm, or visit the current exhibition in the art gallery. Among the treasures you might see are Gilbert Stuart's portrait of George Washington, Charles Dickens's desk, and Thomas Jefferson's own handwritten copy of the Declaration of Independence. Free one-hour tours, each as individual as the library volunteer who leads it, are given Tuesday–Saturday at 11 AM and 2 PM. *Tel. 212/930–0800. Open Tues.–Wed. 11–7:30, Thurs.–Sat. 10–6.*

11 Continue east on 42nd Street to **Grand Central Terminal** (not a "station," as many people call it, since all runs begin or end here). Constructed between 1903 and 1913, this Manhattan landmark was originally designed by a Minnesota architectural firm and later gussied up with Beaux Arts ornamentation. Stop on the south side of 42nd Street to admire the three huge windows separated by columns, and the Beaux Arts clock and sculpture crowning the facade above the elevated roadway (Park Avenue is routed around Grand Central's upper story). Go in the side doors on Vanderbilt Avenue to enter

the cavernous main concourse, with its 12-story-high ceiling displaying the constellations of the zodiac. If you can handle it, the best time to visit is at rush hour, when this immense room crackles with the frenzy of scurrying commuters, dashing every which way. *Free tours Wed. at 12:30 PM (meet in front of Chemical Bank inside terminal on main level), tel. 212/935–3960.*

On the southwest corner of Park Avenue and 42nd Street, directly opposite Grand Central, the **Whitney Museum of American Art at Philip Morris** (120 Park Ave.) occupies the ground floor of the Philip Morris Building. Each year this free branch of the Whitney Museum (*see* Tour 3, *below*) presents five successive exhibitions of 20th-century painting and sculpture. An espresso bar and seating areas make it a much more agreeable place to rest than anywhere in Grand Central. *Tel. 212/878–2550. Admission free. Sculpture court open Mon.–Sat. 7:30 AM–9:30 PM, Sun. 11–7; gallery open Mon.–Wed. 11–6, Thurs. 11–7:30, Fri.–Sat. 11–6. Lectures on Wed. at 1 PM.*

Ask New Yorkers to name their favorite skyscraper and most will choose the Art Deco
12 **Chrysler Building** at 42nd Street and Lexington Avenue. Although the Chrysler Corporation itself moved out a long time ago, this graceful shaft culminating in a stainless-steel spire still captivates the eye and the imagination. The building has no observation deck, but you can go inside its elegant dark lobby, which is faced with African marble and covered with a ceiling mural that salutes transportation and human endeavor.

Although its future seemed in question when publisher Mortimer Zuckerman bought it, laying off many staff members, the *Daily News* is still being produced in the **Daily News Building** (220 E. 42nd St.), an Art Deco tower designed with brown-brick spandrels and windows to make it seem loftier than its 37 stories. Step into the lobby for a look at its revolving illuminated globe, 12 feet in diameter; the floor is laid out as a gigantic compass, with bronze lines indicating air mileage from principal world cities to New York. A small gallery displays *News* photos.

13 The **Ford Foundation Building** (320 E. 43rd St., with an entrance on 42nd St.) encloses a 12-story, ⅓-acre greenhouse. With a terraced garden, a still pool, and a couple of dozen full-grown trees, the Ford atrium is open to the public—for tranquil strolling, not for picnics—weekdays from 9 to 5.

Climb the steps along 42nd Street between 1st and 2nd avenues to enter **Tudor City,** a self-contained complex of a dozen buildings featuring half-timbering and lots of stained glass. Constructed between 1925 and 1928, two of the apartment buildings of this residential enclave originally had no east-side windows, lest the tenants be forced to gaze at the slaughterhouses, breweries, and glue factories then located along the East River. Today, however, they're missing a wonderful view of the United Nations Headquarters; you'll have to walk to the terrace at the end of 43rd Street to overlook the UN. This will place you at the head of the **Sharansky Steps** (named for Natan—formerly Anatoly—Sharansky, the Soviet dissident), which run along the **Isaiah Wall** (inscribed "They Shall Beat Their Swords Into Plowshares"); you'll also look down into **Ralph J. Bunche Park** (named for the African-American UN undersecretary) and **Raoul Wallenberg Walk** (named for the Swedish diplomat and World War II hero who saved many Hungarian Jews from the Nazis).

14 The **United Nations Headquarters** complex occupies a lushly landscaped 18-acre riverside tract just east of 1st Avenue between 42nd and 48th streets. Its rose garden is especially pleasant to stroll in, although picnicking is strictly forbidden. A line of flagpoles with banners representing the current roster of 159 member nations stands before the striking 550-foot-high slab of the Secretariat Building, with the domed General Assembly Building nestled at its side. The headquarters were designed in 1947–53 by an international team of architects led by Wallace Harrison. You can enter the General Assembly Building at the 46th Street door; the interior corridors overflow with imaginatively diverse artwork donated by member nations. Free tickets to most sessions are available on a first-

come, first-served basis 15 minutes before sessions begin; pick them up in the General Assembly lobby. (The full General Assembly is in session from the third Tuesday in September to the end of December.) Visitors can take early luncheon in the Delegates Dining Room (jacket required for men) or eat from 9:30 to 4:30 in the public coffee shop. *Tel. 212/963–7713. Tours offered Mon.–Fri. 10–4:15. 1-hr tours leave the General Assembly lobby every 30 min. Tour admission: $6.50 adults, $4.50 students and senior citizens, $3.50 students in 8th grade and under. Children under 5 not permitted.*

## Tour 3: Museum Mile

*Numbers in the margin correspond to points of interest on the Museum Mile and Central Park map.*

Once known as Millionaire's Row, the stretch of 5th Avenue between 79th and 104th streets has been fittingly renamed Museum Mile, for it now contains an impressive cluster of cultural institutions. The connection is more than coincidental: Many museums are housed in what used to be the great mansions of merchant princes and wealthy industrialists. In 1979 a group of 10 5th Avenue institutions formed a consortium that, among other activities, sponsors a Museum Mile Festival each June. The Frick Collection and the Whitney Museum of American Art are not officially part of the Museum Mile Consortium, but they're located close enough to be added to this tour.

It would be impossible to do justice to all these collections in one outing; the Metropolitan Museum alone contains too much to see in a day. You may want to select one or two museums to linger in and simply walk past the others, appreciating their exteriors (this in itself constitutes a minicourse in modern architecture). Save the rest for another day—or for your next trip to New York.

Be sure to pick the right day of the week for this tour: Most of these museums are closed on Monday, but some have free admission during extended hours on Tuesday evening.

1 Begin at 5th Avenue and 70th Street with **The Frick Collection,** housed in an ornate, imposing Beaux Arts mansion built in 1914 for coke-and-steel baron Henry Clay Frick, who wanted the superb art collection he was amassing to be kept far from the soot and smoke of Pittsburgh, where he'd made his fortune. Strolling through the mansion, one can imagine how it felt to live with Vermeers by the front stairs, Gainsborough and Reynolds portraits in the dining room, canvases by Constable and Turner in the library, and Titians, Holbeins, a Giovanni Bellini, and an El Greco in the living room. Some of the collection's best pieces include Rembrandt's *The Polish Rider* and Jean-Honoré Fragonard's series *The Progress of Love.* You can rest in the tranquil indoor court with a fountain and glass ceiling. *1 E. 70th St., tel. 212/288–0700. Admission: $3 adults, $1.50 students and senior citizens. Children under 10 not admitted. Open Tues.–Sat. 10–6, Sun. 1–6, closed holidays.*

Walk one block east to Madison Avenue and
2 head up to 75th Street to **The Whitney Museum of American Art.** This museum grew out of a gallery in the studio of the sculptor and collector Gertrude Vanderbilt Whitney, whose talent and taste were fortuitously accompanied by the wealth of two prominent families. The current building, opened in 1966, is a minimalist gray granite vault, separated from Madison Avenue by a dry moat; it was designed by Marcel Breuer, a member of the Bauhaus school, which prized functionality in architecture. The monolithic exterior is much more forbidding than the interior, where changing exhibitions offer an intelligent survey of 20th-century American works; the second floor offers, among other exhibits, daring new work from American video artists and filmmakers, and the third-floor gallery features a sample of the permanent collection, including Edward Hopper's haunting *Early Sunday Morning* (1930), Georgia O'Keeffe's *White Calico Flower* (1931), and Jasper Johns's *Three Flags* (1958). Alexander Calder's *Circus,* a playful construction he tinkered with throughout his life (1898–1976), stands near the front entrance. The Whitney also has a branch across from Grand Central

Arsenal, **22**
Bethesda Fountain, **18**
Carousel, **15**
Central Park Zoo, **23**
Conservatory Garden, **11**
Conservatory Water, **21**
Cooper-Hewitt Museum, **6**
The Dairy, **14**
El Museo del Barrio, **10**
Frick Collection, **1**
Guggenheim Museum, **4**
International Center of Photography, **8**
Jewish Museum, **7**
Loeb Boathouse, **19**
The Mall, **17**
Metropolitan Museum of Art, **3**
Museum of the City of New York, **9**
National Academy of Design, **5**
The Pond, **12**
Sheep Meadow, **16**
Strawberry Fields, **20**
Whitney Museum of American Art, **2**
Wollman Memorial Rink, **13**

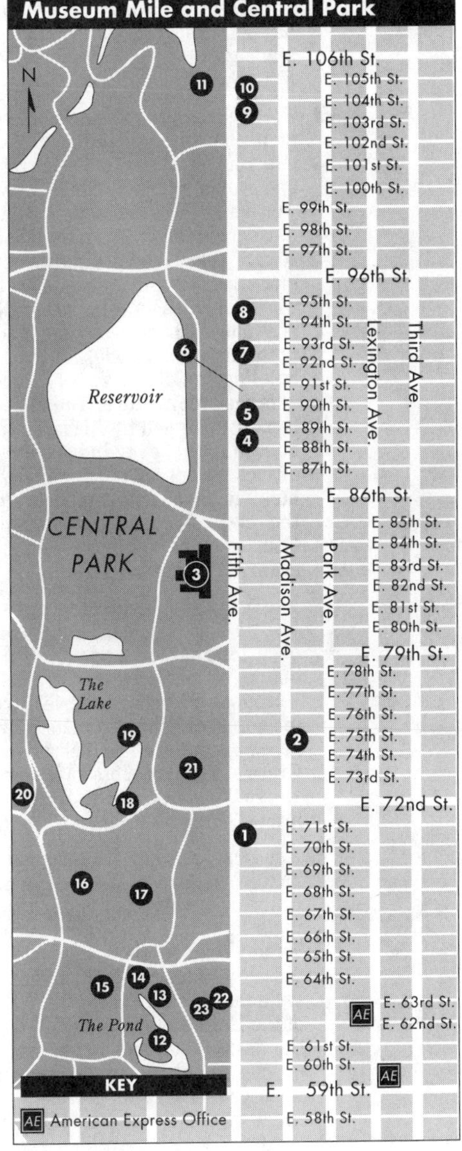

Terminal (*see* Tour 2). *945 Madison Ave. at 75th St., tel. 212/570–3676. Admission: $6 adults, $5 students and senior citizens. Open Wed. and Fri.–Sun. 11–6, Thurs. 1–8.*

3 **The Metropolitan Museum of Art** offers valid evidence for billing itself as "New York's number one tourist attraction"; certainly the quality and range of its holdings make it one of the world's greatest museums. It's the largest art museum in the Western Hemisphere (1.6 million square feet), and its permanent collection of more than 3 million works of art from all over the world includes objects from prehistoric to modern times. The museum, founded in 1870, moved to this location in 1880, but the original redbrick building by Calvert Vaux has since been encased in other architecture. The majestic 5th Avenue facade, designed by Richard Morris Hunt, was built in 1902 of gray Indiana limestone; later additions eventually surrounded the original building on the sides and back. (On a side wall of the new ground-floor European Sculpture Court, you can glimpse the museum's original redbrick facade.)

The 5th Avenue entrance leads into the Great Hall, a soaring neoclassical chamber that has been designated a landmark. Past the admission booths, a vast marble staircase leads up to the European painting galleries, whose highlights include Botticelli's *The Last Communion of St. Jerome*, Pieter Brueghel's *The Harvesters*, El Greco's *View of Toledo*, Johannes Vermeer's *Young Woman with a Water Jug*, and Rembrandt's *Aristotle with a Bust of Homer*.

American art has its own wing, back in the northwest corner; the best approach is on the first floor, where you enter through a refreshingly light and airy garden court graced with Tiffany stained-glass windows, cast-iron staircases by Louis Sullivan, and a marble Federal-style facade taken from the Wall Street branch of the United States Bank. Take the elevator to the third floor and begin working your way down through the rooms decorated in period furniture—everything from a Shaker retiring room to a Federal-era ballroom to the living room of a Frank Lloyd Wright house—and excellent galleries of American painting.

In the realm of 20th-century art, the Met was a latecomer, allowing the Museum of Modern Art and the Whitney to build their collections with little competition until the Metropolitan's contemporary art department was finally established in 1967. The big museum has been trying to make up for lost time, however, and in 1987 it opened the three-story Lila Acheson Wallace Wing, in the southwest corner. Pablo Picasso's 1906 portrait of Gertrude Stein is the centerpiece of this collection.

There is much more to the Met than paintings, however. Visitors with a taste for classical art should go immediately to the left of the Great Hall on the first floor to see the Greek and Roman statuary, not to mention a large collection of rare Roman wall paintings excavated from the lava of Mount Vesuvius. Directly above these galleries, on the second floor, you'll find room after room of Grecian urns and other classical vases. The Met's awesome Egyptian collection, spanning some 3,000 years, lies on the first floor directly to the right of the Great Hall. Its centerpiece is the Temple of Dendur, an entire Roman-period temple (circa 15 BC) donated by the Egyptian government in thanks for U.S. help in saving ancient monuments.

Although it exhibits only a portion of its vast holdings, the Met offers more than can reasonably be seen in one visit. Be aware also that cuts in cultural funding have forced the museum to close certain galleries either mornings or afternoons Tuesday–Thursday; in the course of a day, you can still see anything you want, but ask at the desk for an alternating-gallery schedule to avoid frustration. Choose what you want to see, find a map, and plan your tour accordingly. Walking tours and lectures are free with your admission contribution. Tours covering various sections of the museum begin about every 15 minutes on weekdays, less frequently on weekends; they depart from the Tour Board in the Great Hall. Self-guided audio tours can also be rented at a desk in the Great Hall. Lectures, often related to temporary exhibitions, are given frequently. *5th Ave. at 82nd St., tel. 212/535–7710. Suggested contribution: $6 adults, $3 students and senior citizens. Open Tues.–Thurs. and Sun. 9:30–5:15, Fri. and Sat. 9:30–8:45.*

**Time Out** While the Metropolitan has a good museum café, only a block away is a friendly, sparkling-clean coffee shop: **Nectar of 82nd** (1090 Madison Ave. at 82nd St., tel. 212/772–0916). Omelets, salads, soups, burgers—the portions are generous and the prices quite reasonable.

4 Frank Lloyd Wright's **Guggenheim Museum** (opened in 1959) is a controversial work of architecture—even many of those who like its assertive six-story spiral rotunda will admit that it does not result in the best space in which to view art. Inside, under a 92-foot-high glass dome, a quarter-mile-long ramp spirals down past changing exhibitions of modern art. The museum has especially strong holdings in Wassily Kandinsky, Paul Klee, and Pablo Picasso; the oldest pieces are by the French Impressionists. A new annex called the Tower Galleries opened in June 1992, creating additional gallery space to display the newly acquired Panza Collection of Minimalist art, among other works. The 10-story annex designed by Gwathmey Siegel and based on Wright's original designs offers four spacious galleries that can accommodate the extraordinarily large art pieces that the Guggenheim owns but previously had no room to display. *1071 5th Ave. at 88th St., tel. 212/423–3500. Admission: $7 adults, $4 students and senior citizens, children under 12 free. Joint admission to both branches of the Guggenheim, $10 adults, $6 students and senior citizens. Open Sun.–Wed. 10–6, Fri. and Sat. 10–8.*

5 A block north is **The National Academy of Design,** housed in a stately 19th-century mansion and a pair of town houses on 89th Street. The academy itself, which was founded in 1825, required each elected member to donate a representative work of art, which has resulted in a strong collection of 19th- and 20th-century American art. (Members have included Samuel F. B. Morse, Winslow Homer, John Singer Sargent, Frank Lloyd Wright, and Robert

Rauschenberg.) *1083 5th Ave. at 89th St., tel. 212/369–4880. Admission: $3.50 adults, $2 senior citizens and children under 16; free Tues. 5–8. Open Tues. noon–8, Wed.–Sun. noon–5.*

At 91st Street you'll find the former residence of industrialist Andrew Carnegie, now the home
6 of the **Cooper-Hewitt Museum** (officially the Smithsonian Institution's National Museum of Design). Carnegie sought comfort more than show when he built this 64-room house on what were the outskirts of town in 1901; he administered his extensive philanthropic projects from the first-floor study. (Note the low doorways—Carnegie was only 5 feet 2 inches tall.) The core of the museum's collection was begun in 1897 by the three Hewitt sisters, granddaughters of inventor and industrialist Peter Cooper; major holdings include drawings, prints, textiles, furniture, metalwork, ceramics, glass, woodwork, and wall coverings. *2 E. 91st St., tel. 212/860–6868. Admission: $3 adults, $1.50 students and senior citizens, children under 12 free; free Tues. 5–9. Open Tues. 10–9, Wed.–Sat. 10–5, Sun. noon–5.*

7 **The Jewish Museum** opened its expanded and renovated facilities in June 1993. The expansion preserved the gray stone Gothic-style 1908 mansion occupied by the museum since 1947 and enlarged the 1963 addition. At the same time, the mansion facade was extended, giving the museum the appearance of a late–French Gothic château. The permanent two-floor exhibition, presented alongside temporary shows, traces the development of Jewish culture and identity over 4,000 years. The exhibition draws on the museum's enormous collection of art works, ceremonial objects, and electronic media. *1109 5th Ave. at 92nd St., tel. 212/423–3200. Admission: $6 adults, $4 students and senior citizens, children under 12 free (pay-as you-wish Tues. after 5). Open Sun., Mon., Wed., Thurs. 11–5:45; Tues. 11–8. Closed national and Jewish holidays.*

The handsome, well-proportioned Georgian-style mansion on the corner of 5th Avenue and 94th Street was built in 1914 for Willard Straight, founder of the *New Republic* maga-

8 zine. Today it is the home of **The International Center of Photography** (ICP), a relatively young institution—founded in 1974—building a strong collection of 20th-century photography. Its changing exhibitions often focus on the work of a single prominent photographer or one photographic genre (portraits, architecture, etc.). The bookstore carries an impressive array of photography-oriented books, prints, and postcards. *1130 5th Ave. at 94th St., tel. 212/860–1777. Admission: $4.50 adults, $2.50 students and senior citizens, $1 children under 12. Open Tues. 11–8, Wed.–Sun. 11–6.*

9 **The Museum of the City of New York** traces the course of Big Apple history, from the Dutch settlers of Nieuw Amsterdam to the present day, with period rooms, dioramas, slide shows, and clever displays of memorabilia. An exhibit on the Port of New York illuminates the role of the harbor in New York's rise to greatness; the noteworthy Toy Gallery has several meticulously detailed dollhouses. Weekend programs appeal especially to children. *5th Ave. at 103rd St., tel. 212/534–1672. Suggested contribution: $5 adults; $3 students, senior citizens, and children; $8 family. Open Wed.–Sat. 10–5, Sun. and holidays 1–5; closed Mon., Tues. (tour groups only).*

10 **El Museo del Barrio,** founded in 1969, concentrates on Latin culture in general, with a particular emphasis on Puerto Rican art. ("El Barrio" means "the neighborhood," and the museum is positioned on the edge of Spanish Harlem.) The permanent collection includes numerous pre-Columbian artifacts. *1230 5th Ave. at 104th St., tel. 212/831–7272. Suggested contribution: $2. Open Wed.–Sun. 11–5.*

Having completed this long walk, you may want to reward yourself by crossing the street to Cen-
11 tral Park's **Conservatory Garden.** The entrance, at 105th Street, is through elaborate wrought-iron gates that once graced the mansion of Cornelius Vanderbilt II. In contrast to the deliberately rustic effect of the rest of the park, this is a symmetrical, formal garden. The central lawn is bordered by yew hedges and flowering crab apple trees, leading to a reflecting pool flanked by

a large wisteria arbor. To the south is a high-hedged flower garden named after Frances Hodgson Burnett, author of the children's classic *The Secret Garden*. To the north is the Untermeyer Fountain, with its three spirited girls dancing at the heart of a huge circular bed where 20,000 tulips bloom in the spring, and 5,000 chrysanthemums in the fall.

## Tour 4: Central Park

It's amazing that 843 acres of the world's most valuable real estate should be set aside as a park, yet the city's 1856 decision to do so has proved to be marvelous wisdom, for Central Park contributes mightily toward helping New Yorkers maintain their sanity. It provides space large enough to get lost in (the entire principality of Monaco would fit within its borders), space where you can escape from the rumble of traffic to hear a bird sing or watch an earthworm tumble through the soil.

Although it appears to be simply a swath of rolling countryside exempted from urban development, Central Park is in fact one of the most cunningly planned artificial landscapes ever built. When they began in 1858, designers Frederick Law Olmsted and Calvert Vaux were presented with a swampy neighborhood of a few farms, houses, and a church. It took them 16 years, $14 million, and 5 million cubic yards of moved earth to create this playground of lush lawns, thick forests, and quiet ponds. Hills and tunnels artfully conceal transverse roads (65th, 79th, 86th, and 97th streets) so crosstown traffic will not disturb park goers, and a meandering circular drive carries vehicular traffic in the park (the drive is closed to auto traffic on weekends year-round).

To explore the park on foot, begin at Grand Army Plaza. Enter the park along the main road (East Drive), turning down the first path to your
12 left to the **Pond.** Walk along the shore to the Gapstow Bridge (each of the park's 30 bridges has its own name and individual design), where you can look back at the often-photographed view of midtown skyscrapers reflected in the pond. From left to right, you'll see the peak-

roofed brown Sherry-Netherland hotel, the black-and-white General Motors building, the rose-colored "Chippendale" top of the AT&T building, the black glass shaft of Trump Tower, and in front the green gables of the white Plaza Hotel.

Return to the main path and continue north to
13 **Wollman Memorial Rink,** a skating rink that was once a symbol of municipal inefficiency to New Yorkers. Fruitless and costly attempts by the city to repair the deteriorated facility had kept it closed for years, until real-estate mogul Donald Trump adopted the project and quickly completed it. Even if you don't want to join in, you can stand on the terrace here to watch the skaters—ice-skating throughout the winter, roller-blading and playing miniature golf April through October. The blaring loudspeaker system in this otherwise quiet park makes the rink hard to ignore. *Tel. 212/517–4800. Admission: $6.15 adults, $3.25 children under 13. Skate rental: $3.25. Open daily 10–9:30.*

From April through October part of the rink becomes the **Gotham Miniature Golf** course, where putters maneuver around scale models of various city landmarks. *Tel. 212/517–4800. Admission: $6.50 adults, $3.50 children under 13. Open Mon. 10–5, Tues.–Thurs. 10–9:30, Fri. and Sat. 10 AM–11 PM, Sun. 10–9:30.*

Turn your back to the rink and you'll see the painted, pointed eaves, steeple, and high-
14 pitched slate roof of the **Dairy,** originally an actual dairy built in the 19th century when cows grazed here. Today it's the park's visitor center, offering maps, souvenirs, videos, children's programs, and some very interesting hands-on exhibits. *Tel. 212/794–6565. Open Tues.–Sun. 11–4, Fri. 1–4.*

As you leave the Dairy, follow the path to your right (west) and under the Playmates Arch—aptly named, because it leads to a large area of ballfields and playgrounds. Coming through the arch, you'll hear the jaunty music of the
15 **Carousel.** Although this isn't the park's original one, it was built in 1908 and later moved here from Coney Island. Its 58 ornately hand-carved steeds are three-quarters the size of real

horses, and the organ plays a variety of tunes, new and old. *Tel. 212/879–0244. Admission: 90¢. Open summer, weekdays 10:30–5:30, weekends 10:30–6:30; winter, weekends only 10:30–4:30, weather permitting.*

Climb the slope to the left of the Playmates
Arch and walk beside the Center Drive. From
here you can choose between two parallel
routes: Turn left onto the paved path that runs
16 alongside the chain-link fence of the **Sheep
Meadow,** or go all the way to the circular garden
17 at the foot of the **Mall.** The broad formal walkway of the Mall called **"The Literary Walk"** is a
peaceful spot, lined with the largest group of
American elms in the Northeast and statues of
famous men, including Shakespeare, Robert
Burns, and Sir Walter Scott. The other path,
however, buzzes on weekends with human activity: volleyball games, roller-skating, impromptu
music fests. Watch out for speeding in-line skaters. By contrast, the 15 grassy acres of the
Sheep Meadow make an ideal spot for picnicking
or sunbathing. It's an officially designated quiet
zone, where the most vigorous sports allowed
are kite-flying and Frisbee-tossing. This lawn
was actually used for grazing sheep until 1934;
the nearby sheepfold was turned into the Tavern on the Green restaurant (*see* Tour 5, *below*).

The 72nd Street transverse—the only crosstown street that connects with the East, Center, and West drives—cuts across the park just
north of here, but you can cross it or pass beneath it through a lovely tiled arcade to reach
18 **Bethesda Fountain,** set on an elaborately pat-
terned paved terrace on the edge of the lake.
This ornate, three-tiered fountain is named after the biblical Bethesda pool in Jerusalem,
which was supposedly given healing powers by
an angel (hence the angel rising from the center). Perch on the low terrace wall or the edge of
the fountain and watch the rowboaters stroke
past on the lake. If you want to get out on the
water yourself, take the path east from the ter-
19 race to **Loeb Boathouse,** where in season you can
rent a rowboat. The boathouse also operates a
bike-rental facility and a better-than-average
restaurant. *Boat rental $10 per hr, $20 deposit;
tel. 212/517–4723. Bicycle rental $6 per hr, tan-*

*dems $12 per hr; tel. 212/861–4137. Open May–Oct., daily 11–6.*

Head west on the 72nd Street transverse; on the rocky outcrop directly across the road, you'll see a statue of a falconer gracefully lofting his bird. Turn to the right and you'll see a more prosaic statue, a pompous bronze figure of Daniel Webster with his hand thrust into his coat. Cross the drive behind Webster, being careful to watch for bikes hurtling around the curve.

20 You've now come to **Strawberry Fields,** the "international peace garden" memorializing John Lennon. Climbing up a hill, its curving paths, shrubs, trees, and flower beds create a deliberately informal pastoral landscape, reminiscent of the English parks Lennon may have been thinking of when he wrote the Beatles song "Strawberry Fields Forever" in 1967. A black-and-white mosaic set into one of the sidewalks contains simply the word "Imagine," another Lennon song title. Just beyond the trees, at 72nd Street and Central Park West, is the Dakota (*see* Tour 5, *below*), where Lennon and his wife, Yoko Ono, lived at the time of his death in 1980.

Head back east on 72nd Street drive to one of the park's most formal areas: the symmetrical
21 stone basin of the **Conservatory Water,** where you can watch some very sophisticated model boats being raced each Saturday morning at 10. (Unfortunately, model boats are not for rent here.) At the north end of the pond is one of the park's most beloved statues, José de Creeft's 1960 bronze sculpture of **Alice in Wonderland,** sitting on a giant mushroom with the Mad Hatter, White Rabbit, and leering Cheshire Cat in attendance. Children are encouraged to clamber all over it. On the west side of the pond, a bronze statue of **Hans Christian Andersen,** the Ugly Duckling at his feet, is the site of storytelling hours on summer weekends.

Climb the hill at the far end of the Conservatory Water, cross the 72nd Street transverse, and follow the path south to the Children's Zoo, oft-threatened by city budget cuts and currently closed pending reconstruction. Pass under the Denesmouth Arch to the **Delacorte Clock,** a de-

lightful glockenspiel set above a redbrick arch. Every hour its six-animal band circles around and plays a tune while monkeys on the top hammer their bells. A path to the left will take you
22 around to the front entrance of the **Arsenal**, the Parks Department's headquarters, occupying what was a pre–Civil War arsenal. Since the city acquired it in 1857, it has served as, among other things, the first home of the American Museum of Natural History, now on Central Park West at 79th Street (*see* Tour 5, *below*). The downstairs lobby has some WPA-era great murals; an upstairs gallery features changing exhibitions, often of great interest to kids. *Tel. 212/360–8163. Open weekdays 9:30–4:30.*

23 Just past the clock is the **Central Park Zoo**, recently renamed the **Central Park Wildlife Conservation Center**, a small but delightful menagerie. Clustered around the central Sea Lion Pool are separate exhibits for each of the earth's major environments; the Polar Circle features a huge penguin tank and polar-bear floe; the open-air Temperate Territory is highlighted by a pit of chattering monkeys; and the Tropic Zone contains the flora and fauna of a miniature rain forest. This is a good zoo for children and adults who like to take time to watch the animals; even a leisurely visit will take only about an hour, for there are only about 100 species on display. Go to the Bronx Zoo (*see* Other Attractions, *below*) if you need tigers, giraffes, and elephants—the biggest specimens here are the polar bears. *Tel. 212/439–6500. Admission: $2.50 adults, $1.25 senior citizens, 50¢ children 3–12. No children under 16 allowed in without adult. Open Apr.–Oct., Mon. and Wed.–Fri. 10–4:30, Tues. 10–7, weekends and holidays 10–5; Nov.–Mar., daily 10–4.*

## Tour 5: The Upper West Side

*Numbers in the margin correspond to points of interest on the Upper West Side map.*

The Upper West Side has never been as fashionable as the East Side, despite the fact that it has a similar mix of real estate—large apartment buildings along Central Park West, West End Avenue, and Riverside Drive, and town houses on the shady, quiet cross streets. Once a haven for the Jewish intelligentsia, by the 1960s the West Side had become a rather grungy multiethnic community. In the 1970s gentrification began slowly, with actors, writers, and gays as the earliest settlers. Today, however, this area is quite desirable, with lots of restored brownstones and high-priced co-op apartments.

When you pass **The Ballet Shop** (1887 Broadway, between 61st and 62nd Sts.), a mecca for balletomanes searching for books, prints, and recordings, you'll know you're getting close to New York's major site for the performing arts:
1 **Lincoln Center,** covering an eight-block area west of Broadway between 62nd and 66th streets. This unified complex of pale travertine marble was built during the 1960s to supplant an urban ghetto (*West Side Story* was filmed on the slum's gritty, deserted streets just before the demolition crews moved in). Lincoln Center can seat nearly 18,000 spectators at one time in its various halls (*see* Chapter 6).

Stand on Broadway, facing the central court with its huge fountain. The three concert halls on this plaza clearly relate to one another architecturally, with their symmetrical bilevel facades, yet each has slightly different lines and different details. To your left, huge honeycomb lights hang on the portico of the **New York State Theater,** home to the New York City Ballet and the New York City Opera. Straight ahead, at the rear of the plaza, is the **Metropolitan Opera House,** its brilliant-colored Chagall tapestries visible through the arched lobby windows; the Metropolitan Opera and American Ballet Theatre perform here. To your right, abstract bronze sculptures distinguish **Avery Fisher Hall,** host to the New York Philharmonic Orchestra.

Wander through the plaza, then angle to your left between the New York State Theater and the Metropolitan Opera House into **Damrosch Park,** where summer open-air festivals are often accompanied by free concerts at the **Guggenheim Bandshell.** Angle to your right from the plaza, between the Metropolitan and Avery Fisher, and you'll come to the North Plaza, with a massive Henry Moore sculpture reclining in a

American Museum of Natural History, **4**
Barnard College, **7**
Cathedral of St. John the Divine, **5**
Columbia University, **6**
The Dakota, **3**
Grant's Tomb, **8**
Hayden Planetarium, **4**
Lincoln Center, **1**
Museum of American Folk Art, **2**
Riverside Church, **9**

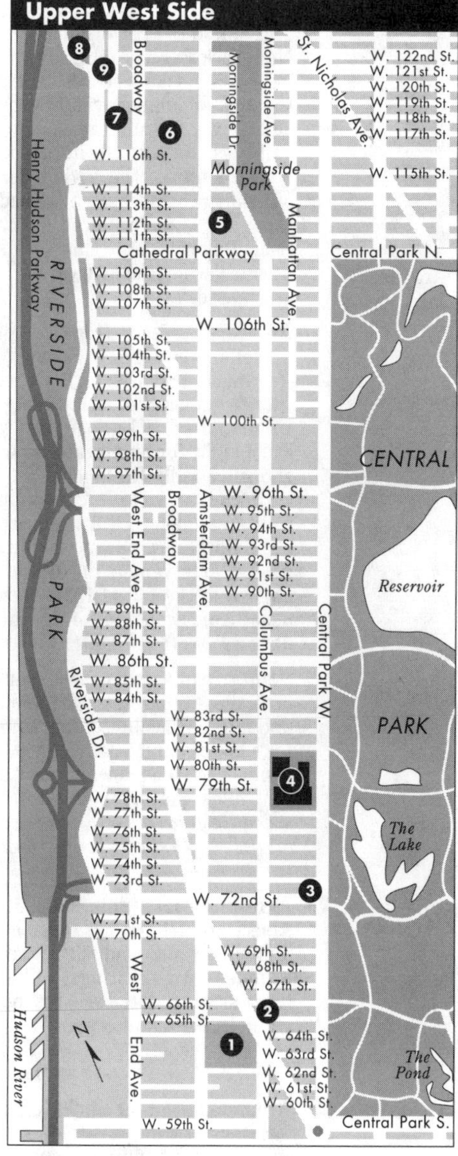

reflecting pool. To the rear is the **Library and Museum of the Performing Arts,** a branch of the New York Public Library with an extensive collection of books, records, and scores on music, theater, and dance; visitors can listen to any of 50,000 records and tapes, or check out its four galleries. Next to the library is the wide glass-walled lobby of the **Vivian Beaumont Theater,** officially considered a Broadway house although it is far removed from the theater district. Below it is the smaller **Mitzi E. Newhouse Theater,** where many award-winning plays have originated.

An overpass leads from this plaza across 65th Street to the world-renowned **Juilliard School** (for music and theater). Check here to see if there's a concert or a play going on; actors Kevin Kline and Patti LuPone once performed here. Turn right for an elevator down to street level and **Alice Tully Hall,** home of the Chamber Music Society of Lincoln Center and the New York Film Festival. Or turn left from the overpass and follow the walkway west to Lincoln Center's newest arts venue, the **Walter Reade Theater,** opened in the fall of 1991, showing several unusual American and foreign films a day, seven days a week (*see* Chapter 6).

Visitors can wander freely through the lobbies of all these buildings. A one-hour guided "Introduction to Lincoln Center" tour covers the center's history and wealth of artworks and usually visits the three principal theaters, performance schedules permitting. *Tel. 212/875–5350 for schedule and reservations. Admission: $7.75 adults, $6.75 students and senior citizens, $4.50 children 6–12.*

2 Across the busy intersection, the **Museum of American Folk Art** has found a new home at Columbus Avenue and 66th Street. Its collection includes naïve paintings, quilts, carvings, dolls, trade signs, painted wood carousel horses, and a giant Indian-chief copper weathervane. *2 Lincoln Sq., tel. 212/977–7298. Suggested contribution: $2. Open Tues.–Sun. 11:30–7:30.*

Around the corner on 66th Street is the headquarters of the ABC television network; ABC owns several buildings along Columbus Avenue as well, including some studios where news shows and soap operas are filmed, so keep an eye out for your favorite daytime doctors, tycoons, and temptresses.

Turn onto West 67th Street and head toward Central Park along one of the city's most handsome blocks. Many of the apartment buildings here were designed as "studio buildings," with immense windows that make them ideal for artists; look up at the facades and imagine the high-ceilinged spaces within. Also notice the Gothic motifs, carved in white stone or wrought in iron, that decorate several of these buildings at street level. Perhaps the finest apartment building on the block is the **Hotel des Artistes** (1 W. 67th St.), built in 1918, with its elaborate mock-Elizabethan lobby. Its tenants have included Isadora Duncan, Rudolph Valentino, Norman Rockwell, Noël Coward, Fannie Hurst, and contemporary actors Joel Grey and Richard Thomas and artist Leroy Neiman; another tenant, Howard Chandler Christy, designed the lush, soft-toned murals in the excellent ground-floor restaurant, **Café des Artistes** (*see* Chapter 4), where Louis Malle's *My Dinner with André* was filmed.

Another dining landmark is just inside Central Park at 66th Street, **Tavern on the Green.** Originally built as a sheepfold, in the days when sheep grazed on the meadows of the park, it was converted into a restaurant in the 1930s. True, the high tone is not what it once was, but many of its dining rooms have fine park views; at night white lights strung through the surrounding trees create a magical effect.

Continue up Central Park West to 72nd Street,
3 where the stately **Dakota** presides over the northwest corner. Its tenants have included Boris Karloff, Judy Holliday, José Ferrer and Rosemary Clooney, Lauren Bacall, Rex Reed, and Gilda Radner. Resembling a buff-colored castle, with copper turrets, its slightly spooky appearance was played up in the movie *Rosemary's Baby,* which was filmed here. Stop by the gate on 72nd Street; this is the spot where, in December 1980, a deranged fan shot John Lennon as he came home from a recording session. Lennon is memorialized in Central

Park's Strawberry Fields, across the street (*see* Tour 4, *above*).

Proceed up Central Park West and you'll see several other famous apartment buildings, including **The Langham** (135 Central Park West), where Mia Farrow's apartment was featured in Woody Allen's film *Hannah and Her Sisters;* the twin-towered **San Remo** (145–146 Central Park West), over the years home to Rita Hayworth, Dustin Hoffman, Raquel Welch, Paul Simon, Tony Randall, and Diane Keaton—but not to Madonna, whose application was rejected because of her flamboyant lifestyle; and **The Kenilworth** (151 Central Park), with its immense pair of ornate front columns, once home to Basil Rathbone, film's quintessential Sherlock Holmes.

4 The **American Museum of Natural History,** the attached **Hayden Planetarium,** and their surrounding grounds occupy a four-block tract bounded by Central Park West, Columbus Avenue, and 77th and 81st streets. As you approach at 77th Street, you can see the original architecture in the pink granite corner towers, with their beehive crowns. A more classical facade was added along Central Park West, with its centerpiece an enormous equestrian statue of President Theodore Roosevelt, naturalist and explorer.

With a collection of more than 30 million artifacts, the museum displays something for every taste, from a 94-foot blue whale to the 563-carat Star of India sapphire. Among the most enduringly popular exhibits are the wondrously detailed dioramas of animal habitat groups, on the first and second floors just behind the rotunda, and the fourth-floor halls full of dinosaur skeletons. A five-story-tall cast of *Barosaurus* rears on its hind legs in the Roosevelt Rotunda, protecting its fossilized baby from a fossil allosaur. The Hall of Human Biology and Evolution, which opened in April 1993, investigates the workings of the human body and features a computerized archaeological dig and an electronic newspaper about human evolution. The Naturemax Theater projects films on a giant screen; the Hayden Planetarium (on 81st

Street) has two stories of exhibits, plus several different Sky Shows projected on 22 wraparound screens; its rock-music laser shows draw crowds of teenagers on Friday and Saturday nights. *Museum: tel. 212/769–5100. Suggested contribution: $5 adults, $2.50 children. Open Sun.–Thurs. 10–5:45; Fri.–Sat. 10–8:45. Planetarium: tel. 212/769–5920. Admission: $5 adults, $3.75 senior citizens and students; $2.50 children 2–12; $7 for laser show. Open weekdays 12:30–4:45, Sat. 10–5:45, Sun. noon–5:45. Naturemax Theater film admission: $5 adults, $3.75 senior citizens and students, $2.50 children. Call 212/769–5650 for show times.*

Take a cab or the Amsterdam Avenue bus up
5 112th Street and stop at the **Cathedral of St. John the Divine,** New York's major Episcopal church. When it is completed, it will be the largest cathedral in the world (St. Peter's of Rome is larger, but it's technically a basilica). Here you can have a rare, fascinating look at a Gothic cathedral in progress. Its first cornerstone was laid in 1892 and a second in 1925, but with the U.S. entry into World War II, construction came to a "temporary" halt that lasted until 1982. St. John's follows traditional Gothic engineering—it is supported by stonemasonry rather than by a steel skeleton—so new stonecutters, many of them youngsters from nearby Harlem neighborhoods, had to be trained before the current work could proceed on the two front towers, the transept, and, finally, the great central tower. A model in the superb gift shop inside shows what the cathedral might look like when completed, probably quite a few years into the future.

The cathedral's vast nave, the length of two football fields, can seat 5,000 worshipers. The second chapel to your left is the only **Poet's Corner** in the United States. The **Baptistry,** to the left of the altar, is an exquisite octagonal chapel with a 15-foot-high marble font and a polychrome sculpted frieze commemorating New York's Dutch heritage.

At 116th Street and Amsterdam, you can pass
6 through the campus gates of **Columbia University,** a wealthy, private, coed institution that is

New York City's only Ivy League school. The gilded crowns on the black wrought-iron gates serve as a reminder that this was originally King's College when it was founded in 1754, before American independence. Walk along the herringbone-patterned brick paths of College Walk into the refreshingly green main quadrangle, dominated by massive neoclassical **Butler Library** to your left (south) and the rotunda-topped **Low Memorial Library** to your right (north). Butler, built in 1934, holds the bulk of the university's 5 million books; Low, built in 1895–97 by McKim, Mead & White (who laid out the general campus plan when the college moved here in 1897), is now mostly offices, but on weekdays you can go inside to see its domed, temple-like former Reading Room. The steps of Low Library, presided over by Daniel Chester French's statue Alma Mater, have been a focal point for campus life, not least during the student riots of 1968.

Across Broadway from Columbia is its sister in-
7 stitution, **Barnard College,** established in 1889. One of the former Seven Sisters of women's colleges, Barnard has steadfastly remained a single-sex institution and has maintained its independence from Columbia, although its students can take classes there (and vice versa). Note the bear (the college's mascot) on the shield above the main gates at 117th Street. Through the gates is **Barnard Hall,** its brick-and-limestone design echoing Columbia's buildings. Turn right to follow the path north through the narrow but neatly landscaped campus; turn left from the main gate to peek into a quiet residential quadrangle.

Across Riverside Drive, in Riverside Park,
8 stands **Grant's Tomb,** where Civil War general and two-term president Ulysses S. Grant rests beside his wife, Julia Dent Grant. The white granite mausoleum, with its imposing columns and classical pediment, is modeled after Les Invalides in Paris, where Napoleon is buried. Under a small white dome, the Grants' twin black marble sarcophagi are sunk into a deep circular chamber, which you view from above; minigalleries to the sides display photographs and Grant memorabilia. In contrast to this aus-

tere monument, the surrounding plaza features fanciful 1960s-era mosaic benches, designed by local schoolchildren. *Riverside Dr. and 122nd St., tel. 212/666–1640. Admission free. Open Wed.–Sun. 9–4:30.*

Just south of Grant's Tomb, on Riverside Drive
9 at 120th Street, **Riverside Church** is a modern (1930) Gothic-style edifice whose smooth, pale limestone walls seem the antithesis of St. John the Divine's rough gray hulk; in fact, it feels more akin to Rockefeller Center, not least because John D. Rockefeller was a major benefactor of the church. While most of the building is refined and restrained, the main entrance, on Riverside Drive, explodes with elaborate stone carving (modeled after the French cathedral of Chartres, as are many other decorative details here). Inside, look at the handsomely ornamented main sanctuary, which seats only half as many people as St. John the Divine does; take the elevator to the top of the 22-story, 356-foot tower (admission: $1), with its 74-bell carillon, the largest in the world. Although affiliated with the Baptist church and the United Church of Christ, Riverside is basically nondenominational, interracial, international, extremely political, and socially conscious. Its calendar includes political and community events, dance and theater programs, and concerts, along with regular Sunday services at 10:45 AM. *Tel. 212/222–5900. Open Mon.–Sat. 9–5, Sun. noon–4; service each Sun. 10:45.*

## Tour 6: Greenwich Village

*Numbers in the margin correspond to points of interest on the Greenwich Village map.*

Greenwich Village, which New Yorkers almost invariably speak of simply as "the Village," enjoyed a raffish reputation for years. Originally a rural outpost of the city—a haven for New Yorkers during early 19th-century smallpox and yellow fever epidemics—many of its blocks still look somewhat pastoral, with brick town houses and low-rises, tiny green parks and hidden courtyards, and a crazy-quilt pattern of narrow, tree-lined streets.

Several generations of writers and artists have lived and worked here: in the 19th century, Henry James, Edgar Allan Poe, Mark Twain, Walt Whitman, and Stephen Crane; at the turn of the century, O. Henry, Edith Wharton, Theodore Dreiser, and Hart Crane; and during the 1920s and '30s, John Dos Passos, Norman Rockwell, Sinclair Lewis, John Reed, Eugene O'Neill, Edward Hopper, and Edna St. Vincent Millay. In the late 1940s and early 1950s, the Abstract Expressionist painters Franz Kline, Jackson Pollock, Mark Rothko, and Willem de Kooning congregated here, as did the Beat writers Jack Kerouac, Allen Ginsberg, and Lawrence Ferlinghetti. The 1960s brought folk musicians and poets, notably Bob Dylan and Peter, Paul, and Mary.

Begin a tour of Greenwich Village at Washing-
1 ton Arch in **Washington Square** at the foot of 5th Avenue. Designed by Stanford White, a wood version of Washington Arch was built in 1889 to commemorate the 100th anniversary of George Washington's presidential inauguration and was originally placed about half a block north of its present location. The arch was reproduced in stone in 1892, and the statues—*Washington at War* on the left, *Washington at Peace* on the right—were added in 1913. Bodybuilder Charles Atlas modeled for *Peace*.

Washington Square started out as a cemetery, principally for yellow-fever victims, and an estimated 10,000–22,000 bodies lie below. In the early 1800s it was a parade ground and the site of public executions; bodies dangled from a conspicuous Hanging Elm that still stands at the northwest corner of the square. Later Washington Square became the focus of a fashionable residential neighborhood and a center of outdoor activity.

Most of the buildings bordering Washington Square belong to New York University. **The Row,** a series of Federal-style town houses along Washington Square North between 5th Avenue and University Place, now serves as university offices and faculty housing. At 7–12 Washington Square North, in fact, only the fronts were preserved, with a 5th Avenue apartment building

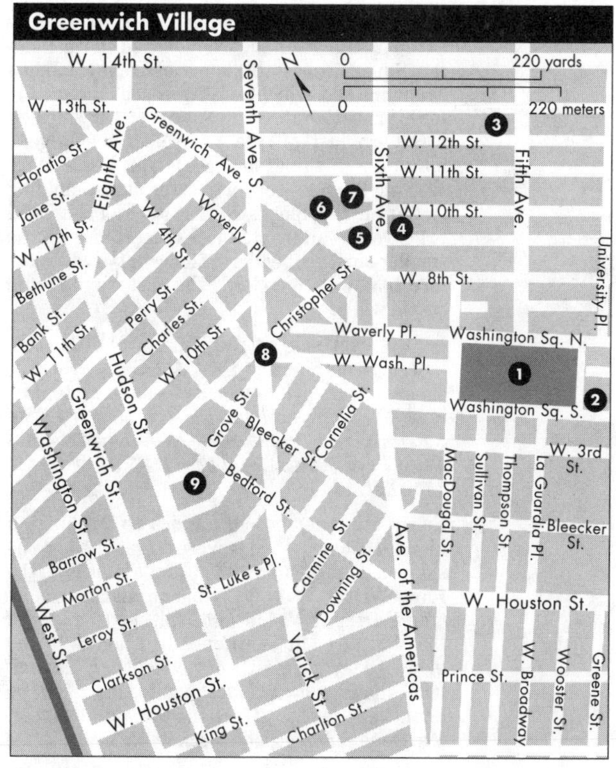


Balducci's, **4**

Forbes Magazine Galleries, **3**

Grey Art Gallery, **2**

Grove Court, **9**

Jefferson Market Library, **5**

Milligan Place, **7**

Patchin Place, **6**

Sheridan Square, **8**

Washington Square, **1**

taking over the space behind. Developers were not so tactful when they demolished 18 Washington Square, once the home of Henry James's grandmother, which he later used as the setting for his novel *Washington Square* (Henry himself was born just off the square, in a long-gone house on Washington Place). The house at 20 Washington Square North is the oldest building (1820) on the block. Notice its Flemish bond brickwork—alternate bricks inserted with the smaller surface (headers) facing out—which before 1830 was considered the best way to build stable walls.

On the east side of the square, NYU's main
❷ building contains the **Grey Art Gallery,** whose changing exhibitions usually focus on contemporary art. *33 Washington Pl., tel. 212/998–6780. Suggested contribution: $2.50. Open Sept.–July, Tues., Thurs. and Fri. 11–6:30, Wed. 11–8:30, Sat. 11–5.*

Go up 5th Avenue half a block to **Washington Mews,** a cobblestoned private street lined on one side with the former stables of the houses on the Row. Writer Walter Lippmann and artist-patron Gertrude Vanderbilt Whitney (founder of the Whitney Museum) once had homes in the mews; today it's mostly owned by NYU. A similar Village mews, **MacDougal Alley,** can be found between 8th Street and the square just off MacDougal Street, one block west.

Walk up 5th Avenue, past the **Church of the Ascension** (5th Ave. and W. 10th St.), a Gothic-style brownstone designed by Richard Upjohn. Inside, you can admire a mural depicting the Ascension of Jesus and stained-glass windows by John LaFarge and a marble altar sculpture by Louis Saint-Gaudens. In 1844, President John Tyler married Julia Gardiner here. Just past
❸ 12th Street, you can stop in the **Forbes Magazine Galleries,** where the late publisher Malcolm Forbes's idiosyncratic personal collection is on display. Exhibits change in the large gallery while permanent highlights include U.S. presidential papers, more than 500 intricate model boats, jeweled Fabergé eggs, and some 12,000 toy soldiers. *62 5th Ave. at 12th St., tel. 212/206–*

*5548. Admission free. Open Tues.–Wed. and Fri.–Sat. 10–4.*

---

**Time Out** If you walk a block east of the Forbes galleries to University Place, you'll find several dining spots located between 8th and 12th streets. At the corner of University Place and 12th Street, **Japonica** (tel. 212/243–7752) serves reasonably priced Japanese lunches, including fresh sushi and excellent sukiyaki. The owners change the restaurant decorations to coincide with the changing seasons and Japanese holidays.

---

Backtrack on 5th Avenue to **West 11th Street** and turn right to see one of the best examples of a Village town-house block. One exception to the general 19th-century redbrick look is the modern, angled front window of 18 West 11th Street, usually occupied by a stuffed bear whose outfit changes from day to day. This house was built after the original was destroyed in a 1970 explosion; members of the radical Weathermen faction had started a bomb factory in the basement. At the end of the block, behind a low gray stone wall on the south side of the street, is the **Second Shearith Israel graveyard,** used by the country's oldest Jewish congregation after the cemetery in Chinatown and before the one in Chelsea.

On Avenue of the Americas (6th Avenue), turn
4 left to sample the wares at **Balducci's** (6th Ave. and 9th St., tel. 212/673–2600), a full-service gourmet food store that sprouted from the vegetable stand of the late Louis Balducci, Sr. Along with more than 80 Italian cheeses and 50 kinds of bread, this family-owned enterprise features imported Italian specialties and a prodigious selection of fresh seafood.

Directly opposite, the triangle formed by West 10th Street, 6th Avenue, and Greenwich Avenue originally held a greenmarket, a jail, and the magnificent towered courthouse that is now
5 the **Jefferson Market Library** (tel. 212/243–4334). Critics variously termed the courthouse's hodgepodge of styles Venetian, Victorian, or Italian; Villagers, noting the alternating wide bands of red brick and narrow strips of granite, dubbed it the Lean Bacon Style. Over

the years, the structure has housed a number of government agencies (public works, civil defense, census bureau, police academy); it was on the verge of demolition when public-spirited citizens saved it and turned it into a public library in 1967. Note the fountain at the corner of West 10th Street and 6th Avenue, and the seal of the City of New York on the east front; inside, look at the handsome interior doorways and climb the graceful circular stairway. If the gate is open, visit the flower garden behind the library, a project run by local green thumbs.

Just west of 6th Avenue on 10th Street is the wrought-iron gateway to a tiny courtyard called
6 **Patchin Place**; around the corner, on 6th Avenue just north of 10th Street, is a similar cul-de-sac,
7 **Milligan Place,** which few New Yorkers even know is there. Both were built around 1850 for the waiters (mostly Basques) who worked at the high-society Brevoort Hotel, long ago demolished, on 5th Avenue. Patchin Place later became home to several writers, including Theodore Dreiser, e.e. cummings, Eugene O'Neill, and Djuna Barnes.

Take Christopher Street, which veers off from the southern end of the library triangle, a few steps to **Gay Street.** A curved lane lined with small row houses circa 1810, Gay Street was originally a black neighborhood and later a strip of speakeasies. Ruth McKinney lived and wrote *My Sister Eileen* in the basement of No. 14, and Howdy Doody was designed in the basement of No. 12. At the end of Gay Street go west on Waverly Place to Christopher Street.

If you continue west on Christopher Street, you'll pass steps leading down to the **Lion's Head** (59 Christopher St.), a longtime hangout for literary types. The restaurant faces a green triangle that's technically called **Christopher Park,** but it contains a statue of Civil War general Philip Sheridan; this confuses New Yorkers, because there's another triangle to the south (between Washington Place, Barrow Street,
8 and 7th Avenue) called **Sheridan Square,** which was recently landscaped following an extensive dig by urban archaeologists, who unearthed ar-

tifacts dating back to the Dutch and Native American eras.

Sheridan Square was the site of a nasty 1863 riot in which a group of freed slaves was nearly lynched; in 1969, gays and police clashed nearby during a protest march that galvanized the gay-rights movement. Across the busy intersection of 7th Avenue, **Christopher Street** comes into its own as the symbolic heart of New York's gay community. Many bars and stores along here cater to that clientele, although the street is by no means off-limits to other people. Two shops worth a visit are **McNulty's Tea and Coffee Co.** (109 Christopher St., tel. 212/242–5351), with a large variety of tea and coffee blends, and **Li-Lac Chocolate Shop** (120 Christopher St., tel. 212/242–7374), a longtime favorite in the area for its homemade chocolate and butter crunch.

West of 7th Avenue, the Village turns into a picture-book town of twisting, tree-lined streets, quaint houses, and tiny restaurants. Follow Grove Street from Sheridan Square past the house where Thomas Paine died (59 Grove St.) and the boyhood home of poet Hart Crane (45 Grove St.).

**Time Out** **The Pink Tea Cup** (42 Grove St., tel. 212/807–6755) is a typical Village restaurant only insofar as it is quirky and one-of-a-kind. Stop here if you have a hankering for down-home hamhocks, chitterlings, or fried pork chops; more standard fare is featured on the menu as well.

At this point, you'll be close to the intersection of Grove and Bleecker streets. You may now choose to take a leisurely stroll along the portion of Bleecker Street that extends west of 7th Avenue from Grove to Bank Street, heading in the direction of Abingdon Square. This section of Bleecker Street is full of crafts and antiques shops, coffeehouses, and small restaurants. Some shopping highlights along the way include **An American Craftsman** (317 Bleecker St., tel. 212/727–0841) for handcrafted gifts; **Pierre Deux** (367–369 Bleecker St., tel. 212/243–7740) and **Susan Parrish** (tel. 212/645–5020) for antiques; **Simon Pearce** (385 Bleecker St., tel. 212/924–1142) for fine glass and pottery; **Biography**

**Bookstore** (400 Bleecker St., tel. 212/807–8655); and **Bird Jungle** (401 Bleecker St., tel. 212/242–1757), with unusual, often colorful species of birds on display in the windows.

If you choose to forego Bleecker Street, continue your walk west on Grove Street. The secluded intersection of Grove and Bedford streets seems to have fallen through a time warp into the 19th century. On the northeast corner stands one of the few remaining clapboard structures in the city (17 Grove St.); wood construction was banned as a fire hazard in 1822, the year it was built. The house has since served many functions; it housed a brothel during the Civil War. Behind it, at 102 Bedford Street, is **Twin Peaks,** an 1835 house that was rather whimsically altered in the 1920s, with stucco, half-timbers, and a pair of steep roof peaks added on.

9 Grove Street curves in front of the iron gate of **Grove Court,** an enclave of brick-fronted town houses from the mid-1800s. Built originally as apartments for employees at neighborhood hotels, Grove Court used to be called Mixed Ale Alley because of the residents' propensity to pool beverages brought from work. It now houses a more affluent crowd: A town house there recently sold for $3 million.

Return along Washington Square South to MacDougal Street and turn right. The **Provincetown Playhouse** (133 MacDougal St., tel. 212/477–5048) premiered many of Eugene O'Neill's plays.

---

**Time Out** The neighborhood's oldest coffeehouse is **Caffe Reggio** (119 MacDougal St., tel. 212/475–9557), where an antique machine steams forth espresso and cappuccino. The tiny tables are close together, but the crowd usually makes for interesting eavesdropping.

---

At **Minetta Tavern** (113 MacDougal St., tel. 212/475–3850), a venerable Village watering hole, turn right onto **Minetta Lane,** which leads to narrow **Minetta Street,** another former speakeasy alley. Both streets follow the course of Minetta Brook, which once flowed through this neighborhood and still bubbles deep beneath the pavement.

The foot of Minetta Street returns you to the corner of 6th Avenue and Bleecker Street, where you reach the stomping grounds of 1960s-era folksingers (many of them performed at the now-defunct Folk City one block north on West 3rd Street). This area still attracts a young crowd—partly because of the proximity of NYU—to its cafés, bars, jazz clubs, coffee-houses, theaters, and cabarets (*see* Chapter 6), not to mention its long row of unpretentious ethnic restaurants.

## Tour 7: SoHo

*Numbers in the margin correspond to points of interest on the SoHo, Little Italy, and Chinatown map.*

Today SoHo is virtually synonymous with a certain postmodern chic—an amalgam of black-clad artists, hip young Wall Streeters, track-lit loft apartments, hip art galleries, and restaurants with a minimalist approach to both food and decor. It's all very urban, very cool, very now. But 25 years ago, they were virtual waste-lands. SoHo (so named because it is the district *So*uth of *Ho*uston Street, bounded by Broadway, Canal Street, and 6th Avenue) was described in a 1962 City Club of New York study as "commercial slum number one." It was saved by two factors: (1) preservationists discovered here the world's greatest concentration of cast-iron architecture and fought to prevent demolition, and (2) artists discovered the large, cheap, well-lit spaces that cast-iron buildings provide. At first it was technically illegal for artists to live in their loft studios, but so many did that eventually the zoning laws were changed to permit residence.

Walk up Greene Street, where the block between Canal and Grand streets contains the longest continuous row of cast-iron buildings anywhere (Nos. 8–34 Greene St.). The architectural rage between 1860 and 1890, cast-iron buildings were popular because they did not require massive walls to bear the weight of the upper stories. With no need for load-bearing

walls, they were able to have more interior space and larger windows. They were also versatile, with various architectural elements produced from standardized molds to mimic any style—Italianate, Victorian Gothic, neo-Grecian, to name but a few visible in SoHo. Look, for example, at 28–30 Greene Street, an 1873
1 building nicknamed the **Queen of Greene Street.** Besides its pale paint job, notice how many decorative features have been applied: dormers, columns, window arches, and projecting central bays. Handsome as they are, these buildings were always commercial, containing stores and light manufacturing, principally textiles. Along this street notice the iron loading docks and the sidewalk vault covers studded with glass disks to let light into basement storage areas. In front of 62–64 Greene Street there's one of the few remaining turn-of-the-century bishop's-crook lampposts, with various cast-iron curlicues from the base to the curved top.

2 At 72–76 Greene Street is the so-called **King of Greene Street,** a five-story Renaissance-style building with a magnificent projecting porch of Corinthian columns. Today the King (now painted yellow) houses the **M-13** art gallery (tel. 212/925–3007) and **The Second Coming,** which sells vintage clothing, furniture, and other curiosities.

Take Prince Street west to Wooster Street, which, like a few other SoHo streets, still has its 19th-century pavement of Belgian blocks, a smoother successor to traditional cobblestones.
3 Start at the **Paula Cooper Gallery** (149–155 Wooster St., tel. 674–0766), one of SoHo's oldest galleries. At 141 Wooster Street, one of several outposts of the DIA Art Foundation, you can
4 visit the **New York Earth Room,** Walter de Maria's avant-garde 1977 artwork that consists of 140 tons of gently sculpted soil filling a second-floor gallery. *Tel. 212/473–8072. Admission free. Open Wed.–Sat. noon–6. Closed Memorial Day–Labor Day.*

At 131 Wooster Street, a store named **Home Town** (tel. 212/674–5770) has the serendipitous quality of an upscale flea market, an eclectic stock of "found objects" and country-style an-

tiques for making trendy lofts feel homey.
5 Across the street is the **Gagosian Gallery** (136 Wooster St., tel. 212/228–2828), operated by prominent uptown dealer Larry Gagosian. The gallery's silver-and-glass front resembles a very wide garage door.

West Broadway (which, somewhat confusingly, runs parallel to and four blocks west of regular Broadway) is SoHo's main drag, and on Saturday it can be crowded with smartly dressed uptowners and suburbanites who've come down for a little store- and gallery-hopping (*see* Chapter 3). In the block between Prince and Spring streets alone there are three major art stops: **420 West Broadway,** with six separate galleries including two of the biggest SoHo names, Leo Castelli (tel. 212/431–5160) and the Sonnabend Gallery (tel. 212/966–6160); the **Mary Boone Gallery** (417 W. Broadway tel. 212/431–1818); and another excellent cluster of galleries at **415 West Broadway,** including the Witkin Gallery (tel. 212/925–5510) for photography. One block south, at **383 West Broadway,** OK Harris (tel. 212/431–3600) has its digs.

---

**Time Out** The crowded, lively **Cupping Room Cafe** (359 W. Broadway, tel. 212/925–2898) specializes in comforting soups, muffins, cakes, and brunch, with excellent Bloody Marys.

---

Go east to Broome Street and Broadway, where, on the northeast corner, you'll see the sadly unrestored classic of the cast-iron genre,
6 the **Haughwout Building** (488 Broadway), nicknamed the Parthenon of Cast Iron. Built in 1857 to house Eder Haughwout's china and glassware business, the exterior was inspired by a Venetian palazzo. Inside, it contained the world's first commercial passenger elevator, a steam-powered device invented by Elisha Graves Otis.

Head north up Broadway, which temporarily loses its SoHo ambience in the midst of discount clothing stores. Just below Prince Street, the 1907 **Singer Building** (561 Broadway) shows the final flower of the cast-iron style, with wrought-iron balconies, terra-cotta panels, and broad expanses of windows. Across the street is one of

Alternative Museum, **10**
Asian American Arts Center, **20**
Chatham Square, **17**
Chinatown History Museum, **16**
Columbus Park, **18**
Confucius Plaza, **19**
Gagosian Gallery, **5**
Grotta Azzurra, **11**
Guggenheim Museum SoHo, **7**
Haughwout Building, **6**
Kam Man, **15**
King of Greene Street, **2**
Museum for African Art, **9**
New Museum of Contemporary Art, **8**
New York Earth Room, **4**
Paula Cooper Gallery, **3**
Puglia, **13**
Queen of Greene Street, **1**
San Gennaro Church, **14**
Umberto's Clam House, **12**

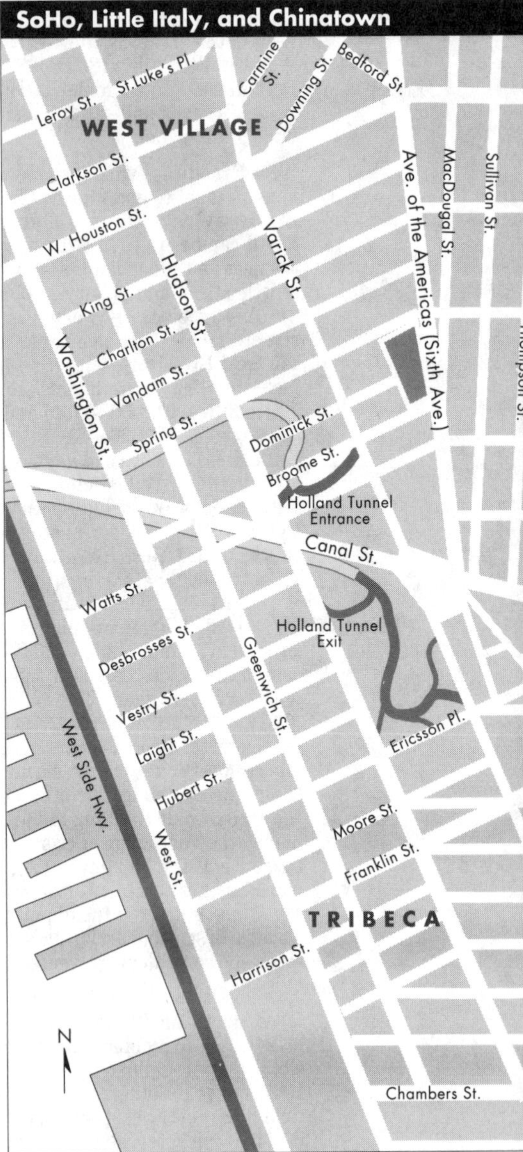

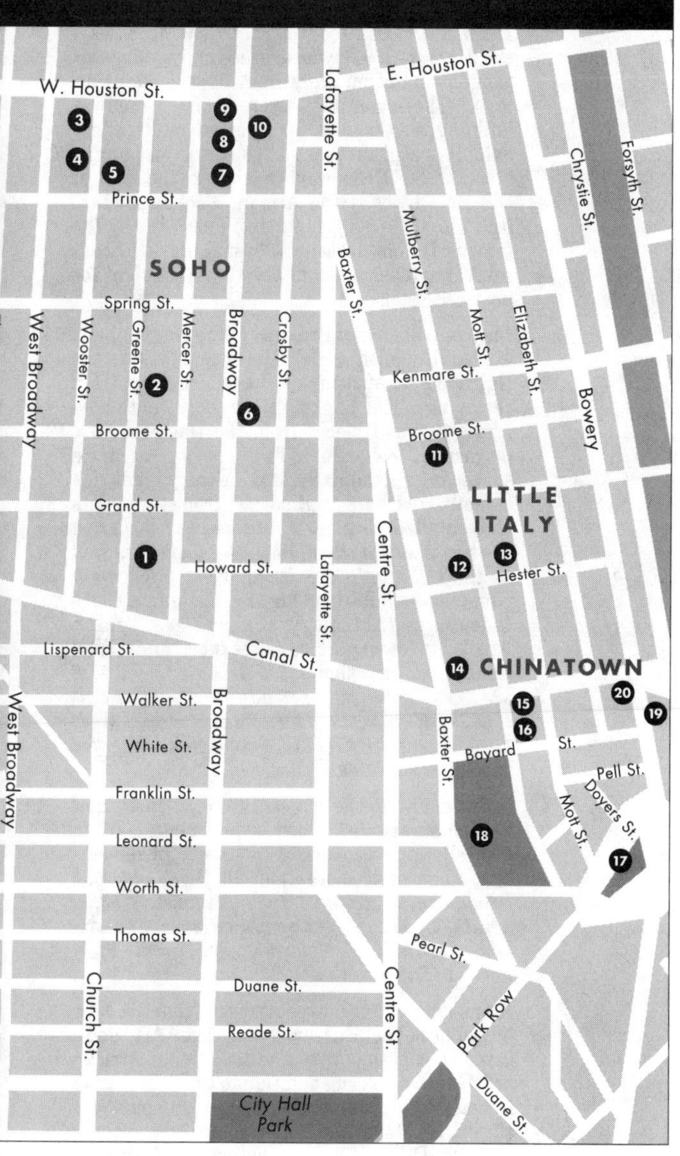

E. Houston St.
W. Houston St.
Lafayette St.
Chrystie St.
Forsyth St.
Prince St.
Mulberry St.
SOHO
Baxter St.
Spring St.
West Broadway
Wooster St.
Greene St.
Mercer St.
Broadway
Crosby St.
Mott St.
Elizabeth St.
Kenmare St.
Bowery
Broome St.
Broome St.
LITTLE ITALY
Grand St.
Centre St.
Howard St.
Lafayette St.
Hester St.
Lispenard St.
Canal St.
CHINATOWN
Walker St.
Broadway
West Broadway
White St.
Baxter St.
Bayard St.
Pell St.
Franklin St.
Mott St.
Doyers St.
Leonard St.
Worth St.
Thomas St.
Pearl St.
Church St.
Duane St.
Centre St.
Park Row
Reade St.
Duane St.
City Hall Park
1
2
3
4
5
6
7
8
9
10
11
12
13
14
15
16
17
18
19
20

New York's gourmet shrines, the gleaming **Dean & DeLuca** food market (560 Broadway, tel. 212/431–1691), whose bread and produce arrangements often are worthy of still-life paintings. The smartly restored **560 Broadway** building also houses a respected multigallery exhibit space; another such space is just up the street at **568 Broadway.** On the ground floor at 568 Broadway is the **Armani Exchange** store (tel. 212/431–6000), featuring a new line by the famous Italian designer—casual, basic clothes several notches up from The Gap, just right for post-recession chic.

On the west side of Broadway, the Guggenheim Museum opened a SoHo branch in 1992: the
7 **Guggenheim Museum SoHo,** which displays a revolving series of exhibitions, both contemporary work and pieces from the Guggenheim's permanent collection. The museum occupies space in a landmark 19th-century redbrick structure with its original cast-iron storefronts and detailed cornice. Arata Isozaki designed the two floors of stark, loftlike galleries as well as the museum store facing West Broadway. Scheduled exhibitions for 1995 include a Claes Oldenburg "Anthology," which goes up in April, following Ross Bleckner and Felix Gonzalez-Torres shows. *575 Broadway, tel. 212/423–3500. Admission: $5 adults, $3 senior citizens and students. Open Sun., Mon., Wed. 11–6; Thurs.–Sat. 11–10. Admission higher for special exhibitions.*

8 A few doors up the street, the **New Museum of Contemporary Art** shows experimental, often radically innovative work by unrecognized artists, none of it more than 10 years old. *583 Broadway, tel. 212/219–1222. Admission: $3.50 adults, $2.50 students, senior citizens, and artists. Open Wed., Thurs., Fri., and Sun. noon–6; Sat. noon–8.*

A few doors up the street (north) from the New
9 Museum is the **Museum for African Art,** dedicated to contemporary and traditional African art. This fascinating addition to the SoHo scene is housed in a handsome, two-story space designed by Maya Lin, who also designed Washington, DC's Vietnam Veterans Memorial.

Exhibits may include contemporary sculpture, ceremonial masks, architectural details, costumes, and textiles. The museum store features African crafts, clothing, and jewelry. *593 Broadway, tel. 212/966–1313. Admission: $3 adults; $1.50 students, senior citizens, and children under 12. Open Tues.–Fri. 10:30–5:30; Sat. noon–8; Sun. noon–6.*

10 Across Broadway, the **Alternative Museum,** a gallery that exhibits art with a political or sociopolitical twist, has moved up to SoHo from its former TriBeCa home. *594 Broadway, tel. 212/966–4444. Suggested contribution: $3. Open Tues.–Sat. 11–6.*

## Tour 8: Little Italy

Mulberry Street is the heart of Little Italy; in fact, at this point it's virtually the entire body. In 1932 an estimated 98% of the inhabitants of this area were of Italian birth or heritage, but since then the growth and expansion of neighboring Chinatown have encroached on the Italian neighborhood to such an extent that merchants and community leaders of the Little Italy Restoration Association (LIRA) negotiated a truce in which the Chinese agreed to let at least Mulberry remain an all-Italian street.

At the southwest corner of Broome and Mulberry streets, stairs lead down through a glass entrance to what seems to be a blue-tiled cave—
11 and, appropriately enough, it is the **Grotta Azzurra** (Blue Grotto) restaurant (387 Broome St., tel. 212/925–8775), a longtime favorite for both the hearty food and the very Italian ambience. Across Mulberry Street is **Caffe Roma** (385 Broome St., 212/226–8413), a traditional pastry shop where you can eat cannoli at postage-stamp-size wrought-iron tables.

At the corner of Mulberry and Grand streets, face north (uptown); on your right you'll see a series of wide, four-story houses from the early 19th century, built long before the great flood of immigration hit this neighborhood between 1890 and 1924. Turn and look south along the east side of Mulberry Street to see Little Italy's predominant architecture today: tenement buildings with fire escapes projecting over the sidewalks. Most of these are of the late-19th-century New York style known as railroad flats: six-story buildings on 25-by-90-foot lots, with all the rooms in each apartment placed in a straight line like railroad cars. This style was common in the densely populated immigrant neighborhoods of lower Manhattan until 1901, when the city passed an ordinance requiring air shafts in the interior of buildings. On the southeast corner, **E. Rossi & Co.** (191 Grand St., tel. 212/966–6640; established in 1902) is an antiquated little shop that sells housewares, espresso makers, embroidered religious postcards, and jocular Italian T-shirts. Down Grand Street is **Ferrara's** (195 Grand St., tel. 212/226–6150), a 100-year-old pastry shop that ships its creations—cannoli, peasant pie, Italian rum cake—all over the world. Another survivor of the pretenement era is at 149 Mulberry Street, formerly the Van Rensselaer House (built in 1816); notice its dormer windows. Today it houses **Paolucci's Restaurant** (tel. 212/226–9653).

12 **Umberto's Clam House** (129 Mulberry St., tel.
212/431–7545) is perhaps best known as the
place where mobster Joey Gallo was munching
scungili in 1973 when he was fatally surprised
by a task force of mob hit men. Quite peaceful
now, Umberto's specializes in fresh shellfish in a
spicy tomato sauce. Turn onto Hester Street to
13 visit yet another Little Italy institution, **Puglia**
(189 Hester St., tel. 212/966–6006), a restaurant
where guests sit at long communal tables, sing
along with house entertainers, and enjoy mod-
erately priced southern Italian specialties with
quantities of homemade wine.

One street west, on Baxter Street toward Canal
14 Street, stands the **San Gennaro Church** (officially, Most Precious Blood Church, National
Shrine of San Gennaro), which each year around
September 19 sponsors Little Italy's keynote
event, the annual Feast of San Gennaro. (The
community's other big festival celebrates St.
Anthony of Padua, in June; that church is at
Houston and Sullivan streets, in what is now
SoHo.) During the feasts, Little Italy's streets
are closed to traffic, arches of tinsel span the
thoroughfares, the sidewalks are lined with
booths offering games and food, and the whole

scene is one noisy, crowded, kitschy, delightful party.

## Tour 9: Chinatown

Visibly exotic, Chinatown is a popular tourist attraction, but it is also a real, vital community, where about half of the city's population of 300,000 Chinese still live. Its main businesses are restaurants and garment factories; some 55% of its residents speak little or no English. Theoretically, Chinatown is divided from Little Italy by Canal Street, the bustling artery that links the Holland Tunnel (to New Jersey) and the Manhattan Bridge (to Brooklyn). However, in recent years, an influx of immigrants from the People's Republic of China, Taiwan, and especially Hong Kong has swelled Manhattan's Chinese population, and Hong Kong residents, anticipating the return of the British colony to PRC domination in 1997, have been investing their capital in Chinatown real estate. Consequently, Chinatown now spills over its traditional borders into Little Italy to the north and the formerly Jewish Lower East Side to the east.

Originally Canal Street was a tree-lined road with a canal running its length. Today the Chinatown stretch of Canal Street is almost overwhelmed with sidewalk markets bursting with stacks of fresh seafood and strange-shaped vegetables in extraterrestrial shades of green. Food shops proudly display their wares: If America's motto is "a chicken in every pot," then Chinatown's must be "a roast duck in every window."

15 The slightly less frantic **Kam Man** (200 Canal St., tel. 212/571–0330), a duplex supermarket, sells an amazing assortment of fresh and canned imported groceries, herbs, and the sort of dinnerware and furniture familiar to patrons of Chinese restaurants. Choose from dozens of varieties of noodles or such delicacies as dried starch and fresh chicken feet.

16 The **Chinatown History Museum,** at the corner of Bayard and Mulberry streets, shows interactive photographic exhibitions on Asian-American labor history. It also has a resource library and bookstore and offers a walking tour of Chi-

natown from April to November. *70 Mulberry St., 2nd Floor, tel. 212/619–4785. Admission: $1. Open weekdays and Sun. noon–5.*

**Mott Street,** the principal business street of the neighborhood, looks the way you might expect Chinatown to look: narrow and twisting, crammed with souvenir shops and restaurants in funky pagoda-style buildings, crowded with pedestrians at all hours of the day or night. Within the few dense blocks of Chinatown, hundreds of restaurants serve every imaginable type of Chinese cuisine, from fast-food noodles or dumplings to sumptuous Hunan, Szechuan, Cantonese, Mandarin, and Shanghai feasts (*see* Chapter 4). Every New Yorker thinks he or she knows the absolute, flat-out best, but whichever one you try, at 8 PM on Saturday, don't be surprised if you have to wait in line to get in.

As you proceed down Mott Street, take a peek down Pell Street, a narrow lane of wall-to-wall restaurants whose neon signs stretch halfway across the thoroughfare. At 35 Pell Street is **May May Chinese Gourmet Bakery** (tel. 212/267–6733), a good place to stop for Chinese pastries, rice dumplings, and vegetarian specialties, such as yam cakes and vegetarian spring rolls.

---

**Time Out** A few steps down Pell Street, turn onto Doyers Street to find the **Viet-Nam Restaurant** (11 Doyers St., tel. 212/693–0725), an informal, inexpensive little basement Vietnamese restaurant that serves spicy, exotic Vietnamese dishes.

---

At the corner of Mott and Mosco streets stands the **Church of the Transfiguration.** Built in 1801 as the Zion Episcopal Church, this imposing Georgian structure with Gothic windows is now a Chinese Catholic church where mass is said in Cantonese, Mandarin, and English. Directly across the street from the church is **Quong Yuen Shing & Co.** (32 Mott St., tel. 212/962–6280), one of Chinatown's oldest curio shops, with porcelain bowls, teapots, and cups for sale.

17 At the end of Mott Street is **Chatham Square,** which is really more of a labyrinth than a square: 10 streets converge here, creating

pandemonium for cars and a nightmare for pedestrians. A Chinese arch honoring Chinese casualties in American wars stands on an island in the eye of the storm.

Skirting Chatham Square, head back to the right to go down Worth Street. The corner of Worth, Baxter, and Park streets was once known as Five Points, the central intersection of a tough 19th-century slum of Irish and German immigrants. Today it has been replaced by
18 **Columbus Park,** a shady, paved urban space where children play and elderly Chinese gather to reminisce about their homelands.

Go back past Chatham Square and up the Bow-
19 ery to **Confucius Plaza,** the open area monitored by a statue of Confucius and the sweeping curve of a redbrick high-rise apartment complex named for him. At 18 Bowery, at the corner of Pell Street, stands one of Manhattan's oldest homes, a Federal and Georgian structure built in 1785 by meat wholesaler Edward Mooney. A
20 younger side of Chinatown is shown at the **Asian American Arts Centre,** which displays current work by Asian American artists. *26 Bowery, tel. 212/233–2154. Admission free. Open weekdays 10–6.*

For some exotic shopping, duck into the **Canal Arcade,** a passage linking the Bowery and Elizabeth Street. A few doors down, at 50 Bowery, you'll see the **Silver Palace** restaurant, worth a peek inside for its Chinese rococo interior, complete with dragons whose eyes are blinking lights.

## Tour 10: Lower Manhattan

*Numbers in the margin correspond to points of interest on the Lower Manhattan map.*

Lower Manhattan doesn't cover many acres, but it is packed with attractions, for it has always been central to the city's networks of power and wealth. It was here that the New Amsterdam colony was established by the Dutch in 1625; in 1789, the first capital building of the United States was located here. The city did not really expand beyond these precincts until the middle of the 19th century. Today Lower Manhattan is in many ways dominated by Wall Street, which is both an actual street and a shorthand name for the vast, powerful financial community that clusters around the New York and American stock exchanges.

Our tour begins at the southernmost point of
1 Manhattan, at the **Staten Island Ferry Terminal** (for subway riders, that's just outside the South Ferry station on the No. 1 line). The **Staten Island Ferry** is still the best deal in town: The 20- to 30-minute ride across New York Harbor provides great views of the Manhattan skyline, the Statue of Liberty, the Verrazano-Narrows Bridge, and the New Jersey coast—and it costs only 50¢ round-trip (you must use quarters in the turnstiles). Boats embark on various schedules: every 15 minutes during rush hours, every 20–30 minutes most other times, and every hour after 11 PM and on weekend mornings. A word of advice, however: While commuters love the ferry service's swift, new low-slung craft, the boats ride low in the water and have no outside deck space. Wait for one of the higher, more open old-timers.

2 To the west of South Ferry lies **Battery Park,** a verdant landfill, loaded with monuments and sculpture, at Manhattan's green toe. The park's name refers to a line of cannons once mounted here to defend the shoreline (which ran along what is currently State Street). Head north along the water's edge to the **East Coast Memorial,** a statue of a fierce eagle that presides over eight granite slabs inscribed with the names of U.S. servicemen who died in the Western Atlantic during World War II. Climb the steps of the East Coast Memorial for a fine view of the main features of **New York Harbor;** from left to right: **Governors Island,** a Coast Guard installation; hilly **Staten Island** in the distance; the **Statue of Liberty** on Liberty Island; **Ellis Island,** gateway to the New World for generations of immigrants; and the old railway terminal in **Liberty State Park,** on the mainland in Jersey City, New Jersey.

Continue north past a romantic **statue of Giovanni da Verrazano,** the Florentine merchant who piloted the ship that first sighted

New York and its harbor in 1524. The Verrazano-Narrows Bridge between Brooklyn and Staten Island—the world's longest suspension bridge—is visible from here, just beyond Governors Island.

Built in 1811 as a defense for New York Harbor,
3 the circular brick fortress now called **Castle Clinton** was, when first built, on an island 200 feet from shore. In 1824 it became Castle Garden, an entertainment and concert facility that reached its zenith in 1850 when more than 6,000 people (the capacity of Radio City Music Hall) attended the U.S. debut of the "Swedish Nightingale," Jenny Lind. After landfill connected it to the city, Castle Clinton became, in succession, an immigrant processing center, an aquarium, and now a restored fort, museum, and ticket office for ferries to the **Statue of Liberty** and **Ellis Island.** The ferry ride is one loop; you can get off at Liberty Island, visit the statue, then reboard any ferry and continue on to Ellis Island, boarding another boat once you have finished exploring the historic immigration facility there. *Ferry information: tel. 212/269–5755. Round-trip fare: $6 adults, $5 senior citizens, $3 children 3–17. Daily departures every 45 min 9:30–3:30; more frequent departures and extended hours in summer.*

After arriving on Liberty Island, you have two choices from the ground-floor entrance to the
4 **Statue of Liberty** monument: you can take an elevator 10 stories to the top of the 89-foot-high pedestal, or if you're strong of heart and limb, you can climb 354 steps (the equivalent of a 22-story building) to the crown. (Visitors cannot go up into the torch.) It usually takes two to three hours to walk up to the crown because of the wait beforehand. Erected in 1886 and refurbished for its centennial, the Statue of Liberty weighs 225 tons and stands 151 feet from her feet to her torch. Exhibits inside illustrate the statue's history, including videos of the view from the crown for those who don't make the climb. There is also a model of the statue's face for the blind to feel. *Tel. 212/363–3200. Admission free.*

Alexander Hamilton Customs House, **6**
Battery Park, **2**
Brooklyn Bridge, **16**
Castle Clinton, **3**
City Hall, **15**
Ellis Island, **5**
Federal Hall National Memorial, **9**
Fraunces Tavern, **8**
New York Stock Exchange, **10**
St. Paul's Chapel, **12**
South Street Seaport Historic District, **13**
Staten Island Ferry Terminal, **1**
Statue of Liberty, **4**
Trinity Church, **11**
Vietnam Veterans Memorial, **7**
Woolworth Building, **14**
World Financial Center, **18**
World Trade Center, **17**

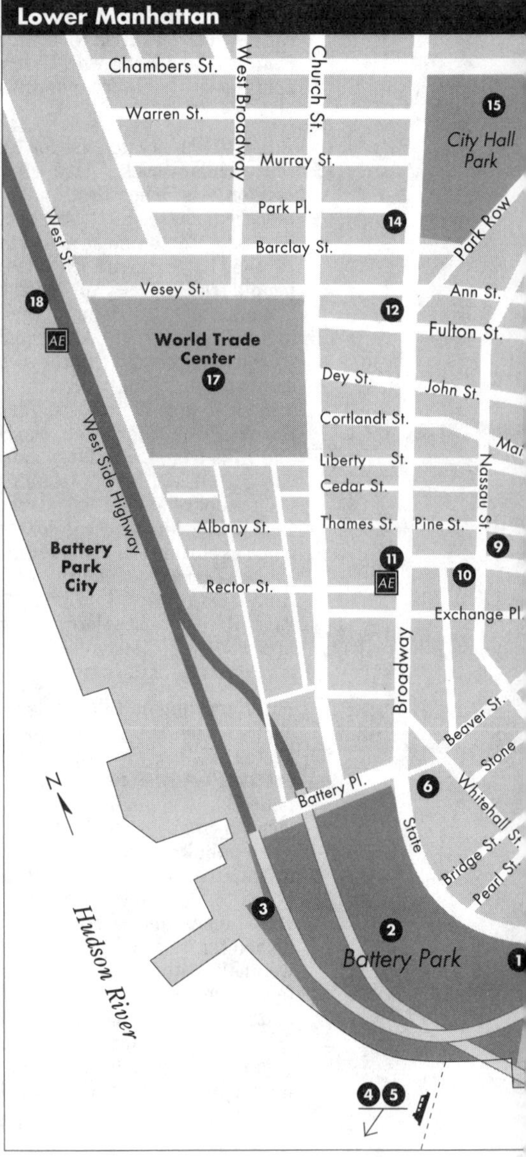

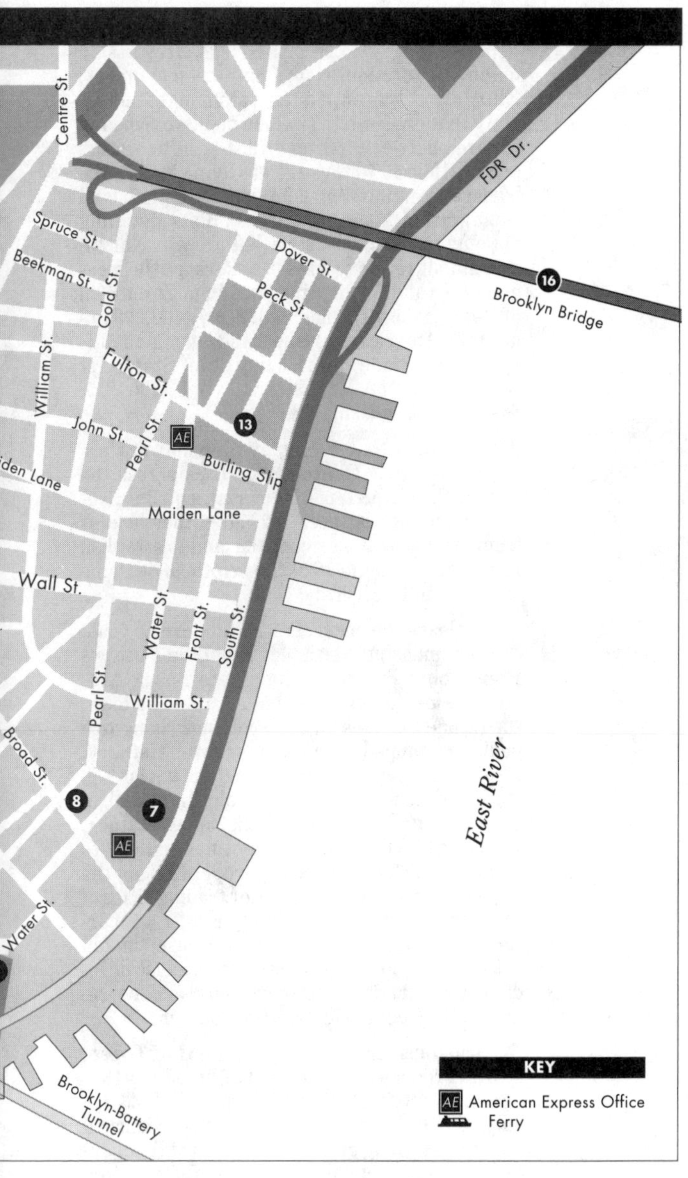
Centre St.
FDR Dr.
Spruce St.
Beekman St.
Gold St.
Dover St.
Peck St.
16
Brooklyn Bridge
William St.
Fulton St.
John St.
Pearl St.
AE
13
Burling Slip
iden Lane
Maiden Lane
Wall St.
Water St.
Front St.
South St.
Pearl St.
William St.
Broad St.
8
7
AE
East River
Water St.
Brooklyn-Battery Tunnel
KEY
AE American Express Office
Ferry

5 The ferry's other stop, **Ellis Island,** opened in September 1990 to record crowds after a $140 million restoration. Now a national monument, Ellis Island was once a federal immigration facility that processed 17 million men, women, and children between 1892 and 1954—the ancestors of more than 40% of Americans living today. The island's main building contains the **Ellis Island Immigration Museum,** with exhibits detailing not only the island's history but the whole history of immigration to America. Perhaps the most moving exhibit is the American Immigrant Wall of Honor, where the names of nearly 400,000 immigrant Americans are inscribed along an outdoor promenade overlooking the Statue of Liberty and the Manhattan skyline. *Tel. 212/ 363–3200. Admission free.*

A broad mall that begins at the landward entrance to Castle Clinton leads back across the park to the **Netherlands Memorial,** a quaint flagpole depicting the bead exchange that bought from the Native Americans the land to establish Fort Amsterdam in 1626. Inscriptions describe the event in English and Dutch.

As you leave the park, across State Street you'll
6 see the imposing **Alexander Hamilton Customs House,** built in 1907 in the ornate Beaux Arts style fashionable at the time. Above the base, the facade features massive columns rising to a pediment topped by a double row of statuary. Daniel Chester French, better known for the statue of Lincoln in the Lincoln Memorial in Washington, DC, sculpted the lower statues, which symbolize various continents (left to right: Asia, the Americas, Europe, Africa); the upper row represents the major trading cities of the world. Federal bankruptcy courts are currently housed in the Customs House; in fall 1994, the National Museum of the American Indian was scheduled to move here and be renamed the George Gustav Heye Center.

The Customs House faces onto **Bowling Green,** an oval greensward at the foot of Broadway that became New York's first public park in 1733. On July 9, 1776, a few hours after citizens learned about the signing of the Declaration of Independence, rioters toppled a statue of British King

George III that had occupied the spot for 11 years; much of the statue's lead was melted down into bullets. In 1783, when the occupying British forces fled the city, they defiantly hoisted a Union Jack on a greased, uncleated flagpole so it couldn't be lowered; patriot John Van Arsdale drove his own cleats into the pole to replace the flag with the Stars and Stripes.

From Bowling Green, head south on State Street. A stunning semicircular office tower in reflective glass hugs the bend of the street at 17 State Street. Next door is the **Shrine of St. Elizabeth Ann Seton** (7–8 State St.). What is now the rectory of the shrine is a redbrick Federal-style town house with a distinctive wood portico shaped to fit the curving street. This house was built in 1793 as the home of the wealthy Watson family; Mother Seton and her family lived here from 1801 to 1803. She joined the Catholic Church in 1805, after the death of her husband, and went on to found the Sisters of Charity, the first American order of nuns. In 1975 she became the first American-born saint. Masses are held here daily.

Continue around onto Water Street, passing on your right **New York Plaza,** a complex of high-tech office towers linked by an underground
7 concourse. Just beyond it is the **Vietnam Veterans Memorial,** where letters from servicemen and servicewomen have been etched into a wall of greenish glass.

Return to Broad Street and go one block inland
8 to **Fraunces Tavern,** a complex of five largely 19th-century buildings housing a museum, restaurant, and bar. The main building is a Colonial home (brick exterior, cream-colored marble portico and balcony) built in 1719 and converted to a tavern in 1762. This was the site where, in 1783, George Washington delivered a farewell address to his officers celebrating the British evacuation of New York; later, the building housed some offices of the fledgling U.S. government. Today Fraunces Tavern contains two fully furnished period rooms and other displays of 18th- and 19th-century American history. *Broad and Pearl Sts., tel. 212/425–1778. Admission: $2.50 adults, $1 students, senior citizens,*

*and children under 12. Museum open weekdays 10–4:45, Sat. 12–4.*

---

**Time Out** The brick plaza behind 85 Broad Street is flanked by a variety of small restaurants. Order a take-out meal or snack and eat it out here on the benches, where you can watch busy office workers milling past and enjoy not being one of them.

---

Head up Pearl Street to **Hanover Square,** a quiet tree-lined plaza that stood on the waterfront when the East River reached Pearl Street. This was the city's original printing-house square; on the site of 81 Pearl Street, William Bradford established the first printing press in the colonies. The pirate Captain Kidd lived in the neighborhood, and the brownstone **India House** (1837) used to house the New York Cotton Exchange. Today it holds Harry's at Hanover Square, a vintage Wall Street bar.

Walk inland up Hanover Square to the rounded corner of South William and Beaver streets, where a graceful columned porch marks the entrance to **Delmonico's** restaurant, opened in 1888 on the site of an earlier Delmonico's founded in 1827. A pioneer in serving Continental cuisine, it was *the* place to go at the turn of the century; under different ownership, it is still a restaurant today.

Two blocks farther north, William Street crosses **Wall Street,** so called because it traces the course of a wood wall built across the island in 1653 to defend the Dutch colony against the native Indians. Although only a third of a mile long, Wall Street began its financial career with stock traders conducting business along the sidewalks or at tables beneath a sheltering buttonwood tree. Today it's a dizzyingly narrow canyon—look to the right and you'll glimpse a sliver of East River waterfront; look to the left and you'll see the spire of Trinity Church, tightly framed by skyscrapers at the head of the street.

To learn the difference between Ionic and Corinthian columns, look at the **Citibank Building** to your right (55 Wall St.). The lower stories were part of an earlier U.S. Customs House, built in 1863, and it was literally a bullish day on Wall Street when oxen hauled its 16 granite Ionic columns up to the site. When the National City Bank took over the building in 1907, the architects McKim, Mead & White added a second tier of columns but made them Corinthian.

One block west on Wall Street, where Broad
Street becomes Nassau Street, you'll find on
your right a regal statue of George Washington
9 on the steps of the **Federal Hall National Memorial.** This 1883 statue by noted sculptor and presidential relative John Quincy Adams Ward marks the spot where Washington was sworn in as the first U.S. president in 1789. After the capital moved to Philadelphia in 1790, the original Federal Hall became New York's City Hall, then was demolished in 1812 when the present City Hall was completed. The clean and simple lines of the current structure, built as (yet another) U.S. Customs House in 1842, were modeled after the Parthenon, a potent symbol for a young nation striving to emulate classical Greek democracy. It's now a museum featuring exhibits on New York and Wall Street. *26 Wall St., tel. 212/264–8711. Admission free. Open weekdays 9–5.*

In building a two-story investment bank at the corner of Wall and Broad streets, J. P. Morgan was in effect declaring himself above the pressures of Wall Street real-estate values. Now **Morgan Guaranty Trust,** the building bears pockmarks near the fourth window on the Wall Street side, created when a bomb that had been placed in a pushcart exploded in 1920.

10 Perhaps the heart of Wall Street is the **New York Stock Exchange,** which has its august Corinthian main entrance around the corner at 20 Broad Street. Compared with the Federal Hall memorial, this neoclassical building is much more elaborately decorated, as befitted the more grandiose national image of 1901, when it was designed. Inside, after what may be a lengthy wait, you can take an elevator to the third-floor visitor center. A self-guided tour, informative slide shows, video displays, and guides may help you interpret the seeming chaos you'll see

from the visitors' gallery overlooking the immense (50-foot-high) trading hall. *Tickets available at 20 Broad St., tel. 212/656–5165. Free tickets are distributed beginning at 9:05; come before 1 PM to assure getting in. Open weekdays 9:15–3:35.*

11 **Trinity Church** (Broadway and Wall St.) was established as an Anglican parish in 1697. The present structure (1846), by Richard Upjohn, ranked as the city's tallest building for most of the second half of the 19th century. Its three huge bronze doors were designed by Richard Morris Hunt to recall Ghiberti's doors for the Baptistry in Florence, Italy. After the exterior sandstone was restored in 1991, New Yorkers were amazed to discover that a church they had always thought of as black was actually a rosy pink. The church's Gothic Revival interior is surprisingly light and elegant, although you may see derelicts napping in the pews. On the church's south side is a 2½-acre graveyard: Alexander Hamilton is buried beneath a white stone pyramid; and a monument commemorates Robert Fulton, the inventor of the steamboat.

12 Head north on Broadway to **St. Paul's Chapel** (Broadway and Fulton St.), the oldest (1766) surviving church in Manhattan and the site of the prayer service following George Washington's inauguration as president. Built of rough Manhattan stone, it was modeled after London's St. Martin-in-the-Fields. It's open until 4 (Sunday until 3) for prayer and meditation; look in the north aisle for Washington's pew.

Walk down Fulton Street, named after the ferry to Brooklyn that once docked at its foot (the ferry itself was named after its inventor, Robert Fulton), to Water Street, which was once the shoreline. On the 19th-century landfill across
13 the street is the 11-block **South Street Seaport Historic District,** which was created in 1967 to save this area from being overtaken by skyscrapers. The Rouse Corporation, which had already created slick so-called "festival marketplaces" in Boston (Quincy Market) and Baltimore (Harborplace), was later hired to restore and adapt the existing historic buildings.

The little white lighthouse at Water and Fulton streets is the **Titanic Memorial,** commemorating the sinking of the RMS *Titanic* in 1912. Beyond it, Fulton Street, cobbled in blocks of Belgian granite, is a pedestrian mall that swarms with visitors, especially on fine-weather weekends. Immediately to your left is the **Cannon's Walk Block,** which contains 15 restored buildings.

At 211 Water Street is **Bowne & Co.,** a reconstructed working 19th-century print shop. Around the corner, a narrow court called Cannon's Walk, lined with shops, opens onto Fulton Street; follow it around to Front Street. Directly across Front Street is the **Fulton Market Building,** a modern building, full of shops and restaurants, that re-creates the bustling commercial atmosphere of the old victual markets that were on this site from 1822 on. On the south side of Fulton Street is the seaport's architectural centerpiece, **Schermerhorn Row,** a red-brick terrace of Georgian- and Federal-style warehouses and countinghouses built in 1811–12. Today the ground floors are occupied by upscale shops, bars, and restaurants, and the **South Street Seaport Museum.** *Tel. 212/669–9400. Admission to ships, galleries, walking tours, Maritime Crafts Center, films, and other seaport events: $6 adults, $5 senior citizens and students, $3 children. Open fall–spring, daily 10–5; summer, daily 10–6.*

Cross South Street under an elevated stretch of the FDR Drive to **Pier 16,** where the historic ships are docked, including the *Peking,* the second-largest sailing ship in existence; the full-rigged *Wavertree;* and the lightship *Ambrose.* A restored **Pilothouse** is the pierside information center. Pier 16 is also the departure point for the 90-minute **Seaport Line Harbor Cruise.** *Tel. 212/233–4800. Fare: $12 adults, $11 senior citizens, $10 students, $6 children. Runs May–Sept. Combination fares—for the cruise and the other attractions—run $15.25, $13.50, $12, and $7.50.*

To the north is **Pier 17,** a multilevel dockside shopping mall. Its weathered-wood rear decks make a splendid spot from which to sit and contemplate the river; look north to see the Brooklyn, Manhattan, and Williamsburg bridges, and look across to see Brooklyn Heights.

**Time Out** If you're hungry, head for the fast-food stalls on Pier 17's third-floor **Promenade Food Court.** The cuisine is nonchain eclectic: Seaport Fries, Pizza on the Pier, Wok & Roll, the Yorkville Packing House, and the Salad Bowl. What's really spectacular is the view from the tables in a glass-walled atrium.

Return along Fulton Street to Broadway and walk two blocks north to the so-called Cathedral of Commerce, the ornate white terra-cotta
14 **Woolworth Building** (Park Pl. and Broadway). When it opened in 1913 it was, at 792 feet, the world's tallest building; it still houses the Woolworth corporate offices. Among its extravagant Gothic-style details are sculptures set into arches in the lobby ceiling; one of them represents an elderly F. W. Woolworth pinching his pennies, while another depicts the architect, Cass Gilbert, cradling in his arms a model of his creation.

Across Broadway is triangular **City Hall Park,** originally the town common. A bronze statue of patriot Nathan Hale, who was hanged as a spy by the British troops occupying New York City, stands on the Broadway side of the park. In its day this green spot has hosted hangings, riots, and demonstrations; it is also the finish line for ticker-tape parades up lower Broadway.

15 **City Hall,** built between 1803 and 1812, is unexpectedly sedate, small-scale, and charming. Its exterior columns reflect the classical influence of Greece and Rome, and the handsome cast-iron cupola is crowned with a statue of Lady Justice. Originally its front and sides were clad in white marble while the back was faced in cheap brownstone, because the city fathers assumed New York would never grow farther north than this. (Limestone now covers all four sides.) The major interior feature is a domed rotunda from which a sweeping marble double staircase leads to the second-floor public rooms. The wood-paneled City Council Chamber in the east wing is small and clubby; the Board of Estimate chamber to the west has colonial paintings and

church-pew-style seating; and the Governor's Room at the head of the stairs, used for ceremonial events, is filled with historic portraits and furniture. The mayor's office is on the ground floor.

Just east of City Hall, a ramp curves up into the
16 pedestrian walkway over the **Brooklyn Bridge.** The Great Bridge promenade takes a half-hour to walk and is a New York experience on a par with the Statue of Liberty trip or the Empire State Building ascent. Before this bridge was built, Brooklynites had to rely on the Fulton Street ferry to get to Brooklyn—a charming way to travel, surely, but unreliable in the fog and ice of winter. After some 50 years of talk about a bridge, John Augustus Roebling, a respected engineer, was handed a bridge construction assignment in 1867. As the project to build the first steel suspension bridge slowly took shape over the next 15 years, it captured the imagination of the city; on its completion in 1883, it was called the Eighth Wonder of the World. Its twin Gothic-arched towers rise 268 feet from the river below. The roadway is supported by a web of steel cables, hung from the towers and attached to block-long anchorages on either shore. It is hardly the longest suspension bridge in the world anymore, but it remains a symbol of what man can accomplish. As you look south from the walkway, the pinnacles of downtown Manhattan loom on your right, Brooklyn Heights stands sentinel on your left, and before you yawns the harbor, with Lady Liberty showing herself in profile. Turn about for a fine view up the East River, spanned within sight by the Manhattan and Williamsburg bridges. You don't need binoculars to enjoy the vistas, but you'd do well to bring a hat or scarf, because the wind whips through the cables like a dervish.

Backtrack across Broadway and turn down
17 Church Street to the **World Trade Center,** a 16-acre, 12-million-square-foot complex that contains New York's two tallest buildings (1,350 feet high). To reach the observation deck on the 107th floor of 2 World Trade Center, elevators glide a quarter of a mile into the sky—in only 58 seconds. The view potentially extends 55 miles, although signs at the ticket window disclose

how far you can see that day and whether the outdoor deck is open. In late February 1993, the Center was the site of a bombing, attributed to terrorists, that killed six people and caused extensive damage to the area. However, the Center has, for the most part, returned to normal operations, though security has been tightened considerably within the complex. *Tel. 212/435–7397. Admission: $4 adults, $2.25 senior citizens, $2 children. Open June–Sept., daily 9:30 AM–11:30 PM; Oct.–May, daily 9:30 AM–9:30 PM.*

Some 50,000 people work in this seven-building complex, and at street level and underground it contains more than 60 stores, services, and restaurants, as well as the adjacent New York Vista hotel. There's a TKTS booth selling discount tickets to Broadway and Off-Broadway shows in the mezzanine of 2 World Trade Center (open weekdays 11–5:30, Sat. 11–1), and on the ninth floor of 4 World Trade Center, a visitors' gallery overlooks the trading floor of the Commodities Exchange (tel. 212/938–2025; open weekdays 9:30–3).

More than a million cubic yards of rock and soil were excavated for the World Trade Center—and then moved across West Street to help beget the 100-acre Battery Park City development, a complete neighborhood built from scratch. Take the pedestrian overpass north of 1 World Trade Center to Battery Park City's centerpiece, the
18 **World Financial Center,** a four-tower complex designed by Cesar Pelli, with some heavy-duty corporate tenants, including Merrill Lynch, American Express, and Dow Jones. You'll come out into the soaring **Winter Garden Atrium,** its mauve marble cascade of steps spilling down into a vaulted plaza with 16 giant palm trees, framed by a vast arched window overlooking the Hudson. This stunning space has become a popular venue for free performances by top-flight musicians and dancers (tel. 212/945–0505). Surrounding the atrium are several upscale shops.

---

**Time Out** While the courtyard also offers several full-service restaurants, for a quick bite head for **Minters** (tel. 212/945–4455)—and be sure to leave room for great ice-cream cones.

---

Of the few spots in Manhattan that directly overlook the rivers, **Battery Park City** just may be the best. The outdoor plaza right behind the atrium curls around a tidy little yacht basin; take in the view of the Statue of Liberty and read the stirring quotations worked into the iron railings. Just north of the basin is the terminal for ferry service to Hoboken, New Jersey (tel. 908/463–3779; fare: $2), on the other side of the Hudson River. It's an eight-minute ride to Frank Sinatra's hometown, with a spectacular view of lower Manhattan.

To the south, a longer riverside promenade that eventually will extend to Battery Park accompanies the residential part of Battery Park City, a mix of high rises, town houses, shops, and green squares that does a surprisingly good job of duplicating the rhythms of the rest of the city. Especially noteworthy among the art works populating the esplanade are Ned Smyth's columned plaza with chessboards; and the South Cove, a collaborative effort, a romantic curved stage set of wood piers and a steel-frame lookout. Slated to open in early 1996 behind South Cove is the **Living Memorial to the Holocaust–Museum of Jewish Heritage** (Battery Pl. between 1st and 2nd Pl., tel. 212/687–9141).

## Other Attractions

In Bronx Park is the **Bronx Zoo,** the nation's largest urban zoo and recently renamed the **International Wildlife Conservation Park.** It deserves nearly an entire day's visit on its own. To get here, take the Liberty Lines BxM11 bus that runs up Madison Avenue (tel. 718/652–8400. Fare: $3.50). At the zoo you'll see two different historical methods of keeping wild animals. The turn-of-the-century zoological garden houses monkeys, sea lions, and elephants (among many others) in fancy Beaux Arts–style edifices at **Astor Court.** It's being gradually replaced by the animal-in-habitat approach used in the **World of Birds,** with its capacious walk-through indoor natural habitats; in **Jungleworld,** an indoor tropical rain forest complete with five waterfalls, millipedes, flowering orchids, and pythons; and in the new **Baboon Reserve.** The **Children's Zoo** ($1.50 admission; open Apr.–

Oct.) features many hands-on learning activities, as well as a large petting zoo. At the **Zoo Center,** visitors will find a rare Sumatran rhino. The zoo as a whole has more than 4,000 animals representing 667 species. *Bronx Zoo, tel. 718/367–1010. Admission: Thurs.–Tues. $5.75 adults, $2 senior citizens and children 2–12 (Nov.–Feb. $2.50 adults, $1 senior citizens and children); Wed. voluntary contribution. Open Feb.–Oct., weekdays 10–5, weekends and holidays 10–5:30; Nov.–Jan., daily 10–4:30.*

**Carnegie Hall** has been hosting musical headliners since 1891, when its first concert was conducted by no less than Tchaikovsky. Outside it's a stout, square brown building with a few Moorish-style arches added, almost as an afterthought, to the facade. Inside, however, is a simply decorated, 2,804-seat auditorium that is considered one of the finest in the world. It was extensively restored before its gala 1990–1991 centennial season, although critics still debate whether the main auditorium's acoustics will ever be as perfect as they were before. The lobby is bigger now, though, and a museum has been added just east of the main auditorium, displaying memorabilia from the hall's illustrious history. Hour-long guided tours of Carnegie Hall are also available. *Carnegie Hall Museum: 881 7th Ave., tel. 212/903–9629. Admission free. Open daily 11–4:30. Guided tours (tel. 212/247–7800) offered Mon., Tues., and Thurs. 11:30, 2, and 3 (performance schedule permitting); admission: $6 adults, $5 students and seniors, $3 children.*

**The Cloisters.** Perched atop a wooded hilltop near Manhattan's northernmost tip, the Cloisters houses the Metropolitan Museum of Art's medieval collection in the style of a medieval monastery. Colonnaded walks connect authentic French and Spanish monastic cloisters, a French Romanesque chapel, a 12th-century chapter house, and a Romanesque apse. An entire room is devoted to a superb set of 15th- and 16th-century tapestries depicting a unicorn hunt. The view of the Hudson River and the New Jersey Palisades (an undeveloped Rockefeller family preserve) enhances the experience. The M–4 "Cloisters–Fort Tryon Park" bus provides

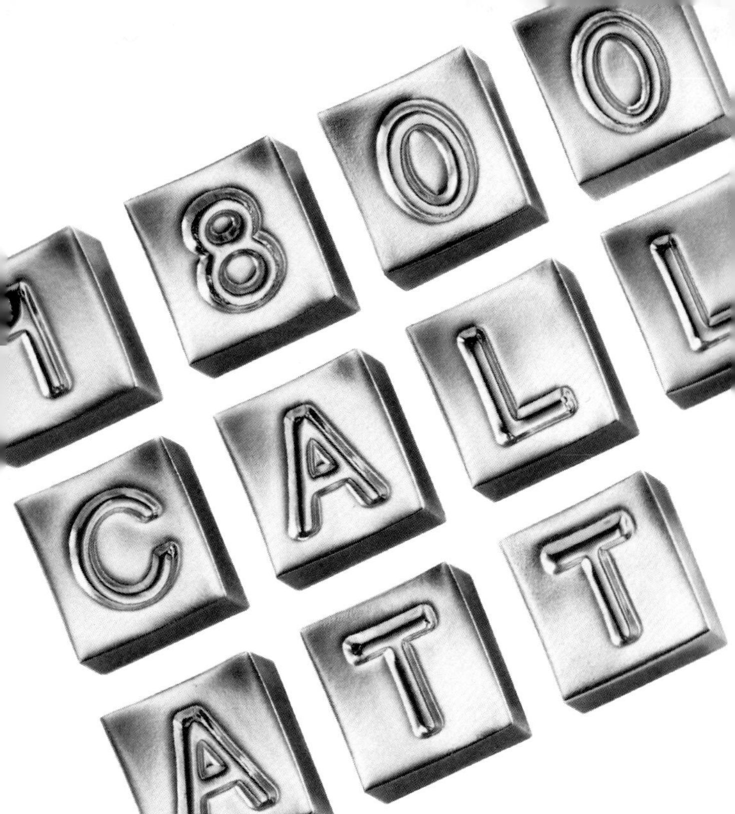


# Pack light.

## Take the one number you need for any kind of call, anywhere you travel.

Checking in with your family back home? Calling for a tow truck? When you're on the road, the phone you use might not accept your calling card. Or you might get overcharged by an unknown telephone company. Here's the solution: dial 1 800 CALL ATT.℠ You'll get flawless AT&T service, competitive calling card prices, and the lowest prices for collect calls from any phone, anywhere. Travel light. Just bring along this one simple number: 1 800 CALL ATT.

AT&T

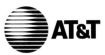

a lengthy but scenic ride; catch it along Madison Avenue below 110th Street, or Broadway above; or take the A subway to 190th Street. *Fort Tryon Park, tel. 212/923–3700. Suggested contribution: $6 adults, $3 senior citizens and students. Open Tues.–Sun. 9:30–5:15. Closes at 4:45 Nov.–Feb.*

The **Empire State Building** may no longer be the world's tallest building, but it is certainly one of the world's best-loved skyscrapers. The Art Deco playground for King Kong opened in 1931 after only about a year of construction. The crowning spire was originally designed as a mooring mast for dirigibles, but none ever docked here; in 1951, a TV transmittal tower was added to the top, raising the total height to 1,472 feet. Today more than 16,000 people work in the building, and more than 2.5 million people a year visit the 86th- and 102nd-floor observatories. Pass beneath the stainless-steel canopy on 34th Street to enter the three-story-high marbled lobby, where illuminated panels depicting the Seven Wonders of the World brazenly add the Empire State as the Eighth Wonder. Go to the concourse level to buy a ticket for the observation decks (here you can also visit the Guiness World of Records Exhibition). The 102nd-floor spot is glassed in; the 86th floor is open to the air. In the movie *An Affair to Remember*, Cary Grant waited here impatiently for his rendezvous with Deborah Kerr. *5th Ave. and 34th St., tel. 212/736–3100. Admission: $3.75 adults, $1.75 children 5–11. Open daily 9:30 AM–midnight; the last elevator up leaves at 11:30 PM.*

**Gracie Mansion,** the official home of the mayor of New York, is located in Carl Schurz Park, which runs along the East River north of 86th Street. Surrounded by a small lawn and flowerbeds, this Federal-style yellow frame house still feels like a country manor house, which is what it was built as in 1779 by wealthy merchant Archibald Gracie. The Gracie family entertained many notable guests at the mansion, including Louis Philippe (later king of France), President John Quincy Adams, the marquis de Lafayette, Alexander Hamilton, James Fenimore Cooper, Washington Irving, and John Jacob Astor. The city purchased Gracie Mansion in

1887, and, after a period of use as the Museum of the City of New York (now at 5th Ave. and 103rd St.—*see* Tour 3, *above*), Mayor Fiorello H. La Guardia made it the official mayor's residence. *Admission: $3 adults, $2 senior citizens. Guided tours mid-Mar.–mid-Nov., Wed. at 10, 11, 1, and 2, by reservation only. Tel. 212/570–4751.*

The **Pierpont Morgan Library** is built around the famous banker's own study and library, completed in 1906 by McKim, Mead & White. Around the corner, at 37th Street and Madison Avenue, is the latest addition to the library, an 1852 Italianate brownstone that was once the home of Morgan's son, J. P. Morgan, Jr. The elder Morgan's own house stood at 36th Street and Madison Avenue; it was torn down after his death and replaced with the simple neoclassical annex that today holds the library's main exhibition space. Turn right just past the entrance and go down a long cloister corridor for the library's most impressive rooms: the elder Morgan's personal study, its red-damask-lined walls hung with first-rate paintings, and his majestic personal library with its dizzying tiers of handsomely bound rare books, letters, and illuminated manuscripts. *29 E. 36th St., tel. 212/685–0008. Suggested contribution: $5 adults, $3 students and senior citizens. Open Tues.–Sat. 10:30–5, Sun. 1–5.*

## What to See and Do with Children

New York is as magical a place for children as it is for adults. For calendars of children's events, consult *New York* magazine and the weekly *Village Voice* newspaper, available at newsstands. The Friday *New York Times* "Weekend" section and the Friday edition of *New York Newsday* also provide a good listing of children's activities.

**Sightseeing** Don't miss the **Statue of Liberty, Ellis Island,** or the **South Street Seaport** (*see* Tour 10), all appreciated by children. Ferry rides are always fun; try the bargain 50¢ ride on the **Staten Island Ferry** (terminal near Battery Park).

**Museums** Although just about every major museum in New York City has something to interest children, certain ones hold special appeal. At the top of the list is the **American Museum of Natural History** (Central Park at 79th St., tel. 212/769–5100), with its lifelike dioramas and giant dinosaurs (partially off-limits until 1995, when restoration of the entire collection will be completed). Also intriguing are the Discovery Room, with hands-on exhibits for children, and the Naturemax Theater, which shows awesome nature films on a gigantic screen. The adjacent **Hayden Planetarium** offers astronomical exhibits and sky shows; there is also a preschool show (reservations required; tel. 212/769–5920) (*see* Tour 5).

The **Children's Museum of Manhattan** is a kind of indoor playground for kids 2–12, with interactive exhibits organized around common childhood experiences. Children can paint, make collages, and try on costumes. *212 W. 83rd St., tel. 212/721–1234. Admission: $4 adults and children, $2 senior citizens. Open Mon., Wed., and Thurs. 1:30–5:30; Fri.–Sun. 10–5.*

The **Children's Museum of the Arts,** in a loftlike space in Soho, allows children ages 18 months to 10 to become actively involved in visual and performing arts. Highlights include the Monet Ball Pond, where children can play with brightly colored balls near a water-lily mural; the Lines and Shapes alcove, where kids have access to computer drawing; and the Creative Play area, which provides a large playpen, a reading corner, art activities, and cushions and futons for relaxation. Weekend workshops are included in the admission price. *72–78 Spring St., tel. 212/941–9198. Admission: $4 adults under 65 and children over 18 months. Admission free, Thurs. 4–7. Open Tues.–Sun. 11–5; Thurs. 11–7.*

Another favorite with the younger generation is the ***Intrepid* Sea-Air-Space Museum,** an immense World War II aircraft carrier. On deck is a startling array of aircraft; inside there are aviation and military exhibits, as well as skinny hallways, winding staircases, and dozens of knobs, buttons, and wheels to manipulate. *Pier 86 at 12th Ave. and W. 46th St., tel. 212/245–0072. Admission: $7 adults, $6 senior citizens* *and veterans, $4 children 6–12. Open Wed.–Sun. 10–5.*

Kids tend to like the **Forbes Magazine Galleries** (62 5th Ave. at 12th St., tel. 212/206–5548) for the collections of toy soldiers and boats, and rooms with the bejeweled Fabergé eggs (*see* Tour 6). Another good bet is the **New York City Fire Museum** (278 Spring St., tel. 212/691–1303), with displays of fire-fighting equipment and tours given by real firefighters.

**Parks and Playgrounds**

In Central Park, children can ride bicycles, play tennis, row boats, go horseback riding, ice-skate, roller-skate, rollerblade, skateboard, fly kites, feed ducks, throw Frisbees, and much more. Favorite destinations include the **Zoo** (*see* Tour 4) and the **Conservatory Water,** which attracts owners of large, remote-controlled model boats and is located near the statues of Alice in Wonderland and Hans Christian Andersen. Younger children enjoy the hands-on activities at the **Dairy** and **Belvedere Castle** (tel. 212/772–0210), as well as an antique **Carousel** (midpark at 65th St., tel. 212/879–0244), complete with painted horses that prance to jaunty organ music; it costs only 90¢ a ride. The **Wollman Rink** (tel. 212/517–4800) has rollerblading and roller-skating classes and sessions—ice-skating in winter—and a **Miniature Golf** course, with obstacles of city buildings.

Manhattan has wonderful state-of-the-art playgrounds. **Central Park**'s adventure playgrounds are full of slides, bridges, bars, swings, towers and tunnels; they're carpeted with sand or soft rubber matting and often cooled in summer by sprinklers, fountains, or running water. Good ones can be found along 5th Avenue at 67th Street near the Zoo, at 71st and 77th streets, and at 85th Street near the Metropolitan Museum. Along Central Park West, the best ones are at 68th, 85th, 93rd (with a Wild West theme), and 96th streets. The large **Hecksher Playground,** midpark at 62nd Street, for toddlers, has good water features.

Also top-rated by Manhattan kids are the playgrounds at **Battery Park City** (West St. south of Vesey St.), **Washington Square Park** (at foot of 5th Ave., between Waverly Pl. and W. 4th St.),

**Abingdon Square Park** (at the triangular junction of Bleecker, Bank, and Hudson Sts. in the West Village), **Carl Schurz Park** (84th St. near East End Ave.), **John Jay Park** (off York Ave. near 77th St., within sight of the East River), and the **Pearl Street Playground** (Fulton, Water, and Pearl Sts.). In **Riverside Park,** west of Riverside Drive, the best playgrounds are at 77th and 91st streets; the one at 77th Street has a circle of spouting elephant fountains. The new **Asser Levy Playground** (23rd St., one block from the East River) is the first in Manhattan that caters fully to disabled children, with giant, multicolored mazelike structures, helter-skelter slides with wheelchair stations, and textured pavement for the blind.

# 3 Shopping

*By Karen Cure*

*Updated by Dick Kagan*

Shopping in New York is theater, architecture, and people-watching all rolled into one. Big stores and small ones, one-of-a-kinds and chains together present an overwhelming array of "Things." There are fabulous department stores, with something for everyone, and tiny specialists.

Another big Manhattan shopping lure is the bargain. Major intersections are instant markets as street peddlers hawk fake Gucci and Cartier watches at $15–$25 each. (These may just possibly last a year or two.) There are thrift shops and resale shops where, it's whispered, Catherine Deneuve snaps up antique lace. At off-price and discount stores, mark-offs are, as locals say, "to die for," and the sales are even better. Designers' showroom sales allow you to buy cheap at the source; auctions promise good prices as well.

Stores are generally open Monday–Saturday from 10 AM to 5 or 6 PM, but neighborhood peculiarities do exist. In midtown and lower Manhattan, shops are often closed all weekend. Most stores on the Lower East Side and in the diamond district on 47th Street close on Friday afternoon and all day Saturday for the Jewish Sabbath while keeping normal hours on Sunday. Sunday hours, also common on the West Side and in the Village and SoHo, are the exception on the Upper East Side.

## Shopping Neighborhoods

**South Street Seaport** The Seaport's shops are located along the cobbled, pedestrians-only extension to Fulton Street; in the Fulton Market building, the original home of the city's fish market; and on the three levels of Pier 17. You'll find some of the best of the country's upscale retailers: **Ann Taylor** and **Laura Ashley** for women's clothing, **Brookstone** for fancy gadgets and hardware, **Caswell-Massey** for fragrances, and **Sharper Image** for high-tech gimmickry.

**World Financial Center** Although the nearby World Trade Center bills its concourse as the city's busiest shopping center, the World Financial Center in Battery Park City is a shopping destination to reckon with, thanks to stores such as **Barneys New York** for clothing, **Godiva Chocolatier** for chocolates,

A & S Plaza, **13**
575 Fifth Avenue, **9**
Barneys New York, **14**
Bergdorf Goodman, **3**
Bloomingdale's, **1**
Galeries Lafayette New York, **5**
Henri Bendel, **4**
Herald Center, **12**
Lord & Taylor, **10**
Lower East Side (Orchard Street), **15**
Macy's, **11**
Manhattan Art and Antiques Center, **6**
Place des Antiquaires, **2**
Rockefeller Center, **7**
Saks Fifth Avenue, **8**
South Street Seaport, **18**
Trump Tower, **5**
World Financial Center, **16**
World Trade Center, **17**

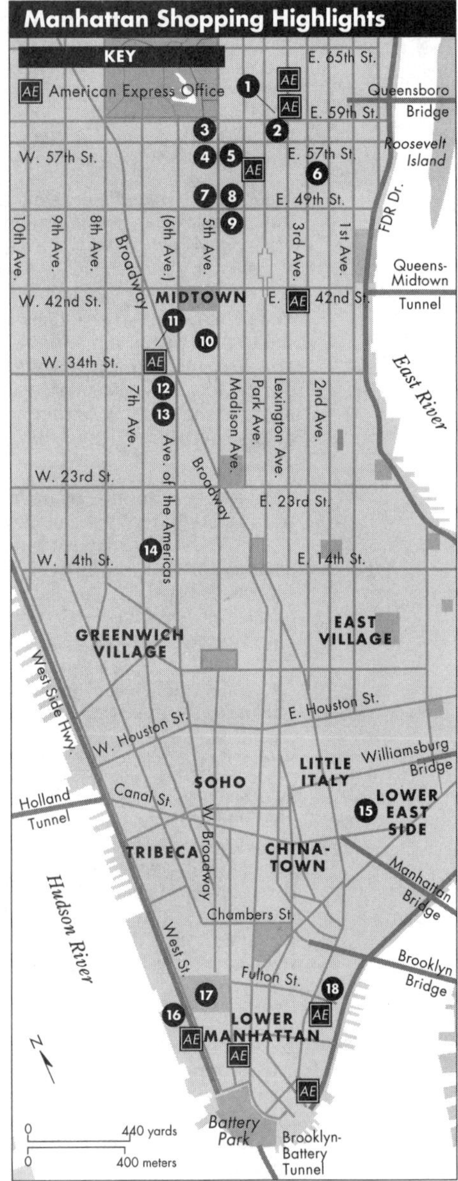

**Mark Cross** for leather goods, **Ann Taylor,** and **Caswell-Massey.**

**Lower East Side** Once home to millions of Jewish immigrants from Russia and Eastern Europe, this area is New Yorkers' bargain beat. The center of it all is narrow, unprepossessing Orchard Street, which is crammed with tiny, no-nonsense clothing and shoe stores ranging from kitschy to elegant.

**SoHo** On West Broadway, SoHo's main drag, and on Broadway and Wooster, Greene, Mercer, Prince, Spring, Broome, and Grand streets, major art galleries keep company with chic clothing stores such as **Yohji Yamamoto** and **Agnès B.**

**Lower 5th Avenue** Fifth Avenue south of 20th Street along with the streets fanning east and west are home to some of New York's hippest shops and a lively downtown crowd. Many of the locals sport clothes from the neighborhood—a mix of **Emporio Armani, Paul Smith,** and **Matsuda** (for Japanese clothing), sometimes finished off with big black shades from **Mikli.** Book lovers head for the enormous outposts of **Barnes & Noble** and its **Sale Annex** on the southeast and southwest corners of 18th Street. **Barneys, Williams-Sonoma,** and **Pottery Barn** are within walking distance on nearby 7th Avenue.

**Herald Square** Reasonable prices prevail at this intersection of 34th Street and Avenue of the Americas (6th Avenue). Giant **Macy's** has traditionally been the linchpin. Opposite is Manhattan's first **Toys "Я" Us.** Next door on 6th Avenue, the **A&S Plaza** atrium mall is anchored by the Manhattan outlet of the Brooklyn-based A&S department store, which makes for wonderful browsing.

**Midtown Near Grand Central** The biggest men's clothiers are here on and just off the stretch of Madison Avenue nicknamed Trad Avenue: **J. Press, Brooks Brothers, Paul Stuart, F. R. Tripler,** and **Wallachs.** Most also handle women's clothing in dress-for-success styles.

**5th Avenue** The boulevard that was once home to some of the biggest names in New York retailing is not what it once was, that role having been usurped by Madison Avenue north of 57th Street. But 5th Avenue from Central Park South to Rockefeller Center still shines with **F.A.O. Schwarz** and **Bergdorf Goodman** (both the main store and **Bergdorf Goodman Men** are at 58th St.), **Tiffany** and **Bulgari** jewelers (at 57th St.), **Ferragamo** and other various luxury stores in **Trump Tower** (all at 56th St.), **Steuben** crystal (also at 56th St.), **Henri Bendel,** across the street, **Takashimaya** (at 54th St.), **Cartier** jewelers (at 52nd St.), and so on down to **Saks Fifth Avenue** (at 50th St.). **Rockefeller Center** itself provides a plethora of shops. To the south (at 47th St.) is the shiny 575 atrium mall, named for its 5th Avenue address, and the venerable **Lord & Taylor** department store (at 39th St.).

**Columbus Avenue** Between 66th and 86th streets, this former tenement district is now home to some of the city's glitziest stores. Shops are mostly modern in design, upscale but not top-of-the-line. Clothing runs the gamut from preppy for men and women (**Frank Stella Ltd.**) to high funk (**Betsey Johnson**) and high style (**Charivari**).

**Upper East Side** On Madison and Lexington avenues, roughly between 57th and 79th streets, New York branches of world-renowned designer emporiums are joined by spirited retailers who fill their stores with the unique and stylish. Domestic and imported items for the home, fine antiques, and wonderful clothing predominate—and the prices aren't always sky high.

## Department Stores

**A&S** (33rd St. and 6th Ave., tel. 212/594–8500). What was the old Gimbel's, a block south of Macy's, lives again as home to A&S Plaza, whose nine floors are anchored by Abraham & Straus, working hard to become as well established here as in the outer boroughs. The sales are some of the best in town.

**Bergdorf Goodman** (754 5th Ave., between 57th and 58th Sts., tel. 212/753–7300). Good taste reigns in an elegant and understated setting. The Home Department is room after exquisite room of wonderful linens, tabletop items, and gifts. The expanded men's store, across the street, occupies the former home of the giant F.A.O. Schwarz toy store (now at 767 5th Ave.).

**Bloomingdale's** (1000 3rd Ave. at 59th St., tel. 212/355–5900). Only a handful of department stores occupy an entire city block; Macy's is one, and this New York institution is another. The main floor is a stupefying maze of mirrors and black walls; elsewhere the racks are overfull, salespeople overworked, and the departments constantly on the move. Still, selections are dazzling at all but the lowest price points, and the markdowns on top-of-the-line designer goods can be extremely rewarding. Exotic special promotions regularly fill the store.

**Galleries Lafayette New York** (4–10 E. 57th St., tel. 212/355–0022). This branch of the French fashion store, opening onto Trump Tower, carries mostly French labels in an upscale assortment of better and designer apparel. Styles here tend more toward youthful than classic.

**Lord & Taylor** (424 5th Ave., between 38th and 39th Sts., tel. 212/391–3344). This store can be relied upon for the wearable, the fashionable, and the classic in clothes and accessories for women. It's refined, well stocked, and never overwhelming.

**Macy's** (Herald Sq., Broadway at 34th St., tel. 212/695–4400). No less than a miracle on 34th Street, Macy's main store is the largest retail store in America. Over the past two decades, it has grown chic enough to rival Bloomingdale's in the style department, but its main floor is reassuringly traditional. And for cooking gear and housewares, the Cellar nearly outdoes Zabar's.

**Saks Fifth Avenue** (611 5th Ave., between 49th and 50th Sts., tel. 212/753–4000). This wonderful store still embodies the spirit of service and style with which it opened in 1926. Saks believes in good manners, the ceremonies of life, and dressing for the part.

**Takashimaya New York** (693 5th Ave., between 54th and 55th Sts., tel. 212/350–0100). This pristine branch of Japan's largest department store carries stylish clothes for women and men and fine household items, all of which reflect a combination of Eastern and Western designs.

## Specialty Shops

**Antiques**

**Manhattan Art & Antiques Center** (1050 2nd Ave., between 55th and 56th Sts., tel. 212/355–4400). More than 100 dealers stocking everything from paisley and Judaica to satsuma, scientifica, and samovars jumble the three floors here. The level of quality is not, as a rule, up to that of Madison Avenue, but then neither are the prices.

**Metropolitan Arts and Antiques Pavilion** (110 W. 19th St., between 6th Ave. and 7th Ave., tel. 212/463–0200). Good for costume jewelry, offbeat bric-a-brac, and '50s kitsch, this antiques mall holds regularly scheduled auctions and specialty shows featuring rare books, photography, tribal art, Victoriana, and other lots.

**Books**

With so many of the country's publishing houses, magazines, and writers based here, there is an abundance of bookshops, small and large. Of course, all the big national chains are here—Barnes & Noble, B. Dalton, Brentano's, Doubleday, Waldenbooks—with branches all over town.

**Biography Bookshop** (400 Bleecker St., tel. 212/807–8655). Diaries, letters, and other biographical and autobiographical material fill this tidy, well-organized store.

**Coliseum Books** (1771 Broadway at 57th St., tel. 212/757–8381). This supermarket of a bookstore has a huge, quirky selection of remainders, best-sellers, and scholarly works.

**Endicott Booksellers** (450 Columbus Ave., between 81st and 82nd Sts., tel. 212/787–6300). This intelligent, wood-paneled bookstore features evening readings once or twice a week.

**Gotham Book Mart** (41 W. 47th St., tel. 212/719–4448). The late Frances Steloff opened this store years ago with just $200 in her pocket, half of it on loan. But she helped launch *Ulysses*, D. H. Lawrence, and Henry Miller and is now legendary among bibliophiles, as is her bookstore, an oasis for those who love to read, with nearly a quarter of a million books.

**Rizzoli** (31 W. 57th St., tel. 212/759–2424; 454 W. Broadway, tel. 212/674–1616; World Financial Center, tel. 212/385–1400). Uptown, an elegant marble entrance, oak paneling, chandeliers, and classical music accompany books on art, architecture, dance, design, foreign language, and travel; the downtown stores come without the fin-de-siècle frills.

**Shakespeare & Company** (2259 Broadway at 81st St., tel. 212/580–7800; 716 Broadway, near Astor Pl., tel. 212/529–1330). The stock here represents what's happening in publishing today in just about every field. Late hours are a plus.

**Tower Books** (383 Lafayette St., tel. 212/228–5100). Owned by the record conglomerate, this megastore discounts thousands of titles; the magazine section alone is worth the visit.

**Crystal**

Three peerless sources are **Baccarat** (625 Madison Ave., between 58th and 59th Sts., tel. 212/826–4100); **Hoya Crystal Gallery** (450 Park Ave., between 56th and 57th Sts., tel. 212/223–6335); and **Steuben** (715 5th Ave. at 56th St., tel. 212/752–1441).

**Food**

**Balducci's** (424 6th Ave. at 9th St., tel. 212/673–2600). In this former mom-and-pop food shop, now one of the city's finest food stores, mounds of baby carrots keep company with frilly lettuce, feathery dill, and superlative meats, fish, cheeses, chocolates, baked goods, pastas, vinegars, oils, and Italian specialties.

**Dean & DeLuca** (560 Broadway at Prince St., tel. 212/431–1691). This huge SoHo trendsetter, splendidly bright white, has an encyclopedic selection, from the heady array at the cheese counter to the shelves of crackers and the display cases of prepared foods.

**Zabar's** (2245 Broadway at 80th St., tel. 212/787–2000). Enjoy the atmosphere of one of New York's favorite food markets. Dried herbs and spices, chocolates, and assorted bottled foods are downstairs, along with a fragrant jumble of fresh breads and the cheese, meat, and smoked-fish counters. Upstairs is one of New York's largest selections of kitchenware.

**Gizmos and Whatchamacallits**

**Hammacher Schlemmer** (147 E. 57th St., tel. 212/421–9000). The store that offered America its first pop-up toaster, the automatic steam iron, telephone answering machine, and microwave oven still ferrets out the outrageous, the unusual, and the best-of-kind.

**Sharper Image** (Pier 17, South St. Seaport, tel. 212/693–0477; 4 W. 57th St., tel. 212/265–2550; 900 Madison Ave., between 72nd and 73rd Sts., tel. 212/794–4974). This retail outlet of the catalogue company stocks gifts for the pampered executive who has everything.

**Jewelry, Watches, and Silver**

Most of the world's premier jewelers have retail outlets in New York, and the nation's jewelry wholesale center is on 47th Street.

**A La Vieille Russie** (781 5th Ave., between 59th and 60th Sts., tel. 212/752–1727). Stop here to behold bibelots by Fabergé and others, enameled or encrusted with jewels.
**Buccellati** (46 E. 57th St., tel. 212/308–5533). The exquisite, Florentine-finish Italian jewelry here makes a statement; as does the silver.
**Camilla Dietz Bergeron** (116 E. 68th St., tel. 212/794–9100). Antique cufflinks here date back to the Roaring '20s. (Open by appointment only.)
**Cartier** (2 E. 52nd St., tel. 212/446–3400). Simple but superb pieces are displayed in the former mansion of the late yachtsman and society king Morton F. Plant.
**Tiffany & Co.** (727 5th Ave. at 57th St., tel. 212/755–8000). A shiny robin's-egg-blue box from this venerable New York jeweler announces the contents as something very special. Along with the $80,000 platinum-and-diamond bracelets, there is a great deal that's affordable on a whim.
**Van Cleef & Arpels** (744 5th Ave. at 57th St., tel. 212/644–9500). The jewelry here is sheer perfection.

**Luggage and Leather Goods**

**Altman Luggage** (135 Orchard St., between Delancey and Rivington Sts., tel. 212/254–7275). Come here for reasonably priced leather items.
**Bottega Veneta** (635 Madison Ave., between 59th and 60th Sts., tel. 212/371–5511). The superb Italian goods here are for people who know real quality.
**Crouch & Fitzgerald** (400 Madison Ave. at 48th St., tel. 212/755–5888). Since 1839, this store has offered a terrific selection in hard- and soft-sided luggage, plus handbags.

**Menswear**

**Alfred Dunhill of London** (450 Park Ave. at 57th St., tel. 212/753–9292). Corporate brass comes here for finely tailored clothing, both ready-made and custom-order, and smoking accessories; the walk-in humidor stores top-quality tobacco and cigars.

**Brooks Brothers** (346 Madison Ave. at 44th St., tel. 212/682–8800). An American-menswear institution, with conservative styles and fine tailoring.

**Frank Stella Ltd.** (440 Columbus Ave. at 81st St., tel. 212/877–5566; 1388 6th Ave., between 56th and 57th Sts., tel. 212/757–2295). Classic clothing with subtle variations is offered here.

**Paul Smith** (108 5th Ave. at 16th St., tel. 212/627–9770). Dark mahogany Victorian cases display downtown styles.

**Paul Stuart** (Madison Ave. at 45th St., tel. 212/682–0320). The fabric selection is interesting, the tailoring superb, and the look traditional but not stodgy.

**Saint Laurie, Ltd.** (897 Broadway, between 19th and 20th Sts., tel. 212/473–0100). This family-owned business sells suits manufactured on the premises in styles ranging from the boxy to the Italianate in lovely fabrics.

**Toys**

**Big City Kite Co.** (1201 Lexington Ave. at 81st St., tel. 212/472–2623). Kites of all sizes and shapes are found here.

**Enchanted Forest** (85 Mercer St., tel. 212/925–6677). Fancy reigns in this shop's stock of unique handmades.

**F.A.O. Schwarz** (767 5th Ave. at 58th St., tel. 212/644–9400). You will be hooked on this sprawling two-level children's store from the minute you walk through the door and one of the costumed staff members—a donkey, a clown, a cave woman, or a mad scientist—extends a welcome. Beyond a wonderful mechanical clock with many dials and dingbats are all the stuffed animals in the world, dolls large and small, things to build with (including blocks by the pound), computer games, toy cars (including a multi-thousand-dollar Ferrari), and more.

**Penny Whistle Toys** (132 Spring St., tel. 212/925–2088; 448 Columbus Ave., between 81st and 82nd Sts., tel. 212/873–9090; 1283 Madison Ave., between 91st and 92nd Sts., tel. 212/369–3868). Meredith Brokaw, wife of TV anchorman

Tom Brokaw, has developed an intriguing selection of quality toys here.

**West Side Kids** (498 Amsterdam Ave. at 84th St., tel. 212/496–7282). The shrewd selection here mixes educational toys with a grab bag of fun little playthings.

**Women's Clothing**

The department stores' collections are always good: **Saks** for its designers; **Macy's** for its breadth; **Bloomingdale's** for its extremes; **Barneys, Galleries Lafayette,** and **Henri Bendel** for their trendy chic; and **Lord & Taylor** for its classicism. The following add another dimension.

*Classicists*

**Ann Taylor** (2017 Broadway, near 69th St., tel. 212/873–7344; 25 Fulton St., tel. 212/608–5600; 805 3rd Ave. at 50th St., tel. 212/308–5333; 3 E. 57th St., tel. 212/832–2010; and other locations). These stores provide what the elegant young woman with a sense of style needs for work and play.

**Burberry's** (9 E. 57th St., tel. 212/371–5010). The look is classic and conservative—and nobody does a better trench coat.

*Designer Showcases*

**Betsey Johnson** (130 Thompson St., tel. 212/420–0169; 251 E. 60th St., tel. 212/319–7699; 248 Columbus Ave., between 71st and 72nd Sts., tel. 212/362–3364; 1060 Madison Ave., between 80th and 81st Sts., tel. 212/734–1257). The look here is still hip and quirky.

**Chanel** (5 E. 57th St., tel. 212/355–5050). The classic designs here never go out of style; neither do those wonderful Chanel perfumes.

**Emanuel Ungaro** (803 Madison Ave., between 67th and 68th Sts., tel. 212/249–4090). The style here is body-conscious, but it's never flashy.

**Emporio Armani** (110 5th Ave., between 16th and 17th Sts., tel. 212/727–3240). The Italian designer's casual line is featured.

**Geoffrey Beene** (783 5th Ave., between 58th and 59th Sts., tel. 212/935–0470). A splendid-looking boutique houses exquisite day and evening wear by America's master designer.

**Giorgio Armani** (815 Madison Ave., between 67th and 68th Sts., tel. 212/988–9191). In this lofty blond-and-beige space with grand, arched windows and doors, Armani's high-end line looks oh-so-chic.

**Missoni** (836 Madison Ave. at 69th St., tel. 212/517–9339). Wonderfully textured knits, suits, and sportswear stand out.

**Nicole Miller** (780 Madison Ave., between 66th and 67th Sts., tel. 212/288–9779). Sexy and colorful, these clothes for a woman by a woman are spirited and sassy.

**Norma Kamali O.M.O.** (11 W. 56th St., tel. 212/957–9797). The look here ranges from sweatshirts to evening gowns.

**Polo/Ralph Lauren** (867 Madison Ave. at 72nd St., tel. 212/606–2100). Lauren's flagship store is one of New York's most distinctive shopping experiences, in a grand, carefully renovated turn-of-the-century town house. The new **Polo Sport** is directly across the street.

**Sonia Rykiel** (792 Madison Ave. at 67th St., tel. 212/744–0880). Signature knits for day and evening pack the racks.

**Valentino** (823 Madison Ave., between 68th and 69th Sts., tel. 212/744–0200). The mix here is at once audacious and beautifully cut, with the best of France and Italy on its racks.

**Yves St. Laurent Rive Gauche** (859 Madison Ave., between 70th and 71st Sts., tel. 212/517–7400). The looks range from chic to classic for day and evening.

*Hip Styles*

**A/X: Armani Exchange** (568 Broadway near Prince St., tel. 212/431–6000). Here's Giorgio Armani's answer to the Gap—with a sleek European touch and a higher price tag.

**Canal Jean** (504 Broadway, between Spring and Broome Sts., tel. 212/226–1130). Casual funk draws hip shoppers.

**Reminiscence** (74 5th Ave., between 13th and 14th Sts., tel. 212/243–2292). The theme is strictly '50s and '60s, in vintage and new clothing.

**Trash and Vaudeville** (4 St. Marks Pl., tel. 212/982–3590). Black, white, and electric colors are the focus here.

**Women's Workout Gear** (121 7th Ave., between 17th and 18th Sts., tel. 212/627–1117). Come here for exercise wear in all colors.

*Trendsetters*

**Agnès B.** (116 Prince St., tel. 212/925–4649). This Euro-style boutique has maintained its SoHo popularity for several years.

**Charivari** (2315 Broadway, between 83rd and

84th Sts., tel. 212/873–1424). Since Selma Weiser founded this store on the Upper West Side, she has made a name for herself internationally for her eagle eye on the up-and-coming and avant-garde. The branches, too, take a high-style approach: **Charivari Sport** (201 W. 79th St., tel. 212/799–8650); **Charivari Workshop** (441 Columbus Ave. at 81st St., tel. 212/496–8700); **Charivari 72** (58 W. 72nd St., tel. 212/787–7272); **Charivari 57** (18 W. 57th St., tel. 212/333–4040); and **Charivari on Madison** (1001 Madison Ave. at 77th St., tel. 212/650–0078).

**Patricia Field** (10 E. 8th St., tel. 212/254–1699). This store collects the essence of the downtown look.

# 4 Dining

*by J. Walman*

*Syndicated travel, food, and wine journalist J. Walman dispenses culinary advice to the 2 million listeners of WEVD-AM, writes regularly for* Chocolatier, *and is president of Punch In International Syndicate, an electronic publishing company specializing in travel, restaurants, entertainment, and wine.*

In most great restaurant towns, there is generally one best restaurant; New York generously offers a variety of candidates. Times being what they are, top restaurants have short lives, chefs play musical kitchens, and today's star is often tomorrow's laggard, so temper your visits to famous restaurants with informed selections from among lesser-knowns.

New York gets a bum rap over its prices. Of course, you can order caviar and champagne or Bordeaux of great years; you will pay accordingly. But you will also do that in Nashville, Chicago, and Los Angeles. Our point is that each price stratum has its own equilibrium. Translation: $20 is only inexpensive if you get $20 of value, and $100 may be a bargain.

If you're watching your budget, always ask the price of specials, which have become a way for restaurants to charge higher-than-normal prices. Finally, always go over your bill. Mistakes do occur (and not always in the favor of the house).

Make a reservation. If you change your mind, cancel—it's only courteous. Dress up for grand restaurants, casually for casual spots. In most restaurants, tip the waiter at least 15% to 20%. (To figure the amount quickly, just double the 8¼% tax noted on the check.)

| Category | Cost* |
| --- | --- |
| $$$$ | over $60 |
| $$$ | $40–$59 |
| $$ | $20–$39 |
| $ | under $20 |

**per person, excluding drinks, service, and sales tax (8¼%)*

The following credit card abbreviations are used: AE, American Express; D, Discover; DC, Diners Club; MC, Mastercard; and V, Visa. Highly recommended restaurants are indicated by a star (★).

## Lower Manhattan

$$$ *American-Contemporary* ★ **Hudson River Club.** Spacious and clubby, with river views and soft piano music, it improves with age. Chef Waldy Malouf celebrates Hudson River Valley produce with his striped bass with fennel and roasted garlic, rabbit pot pie, and apple-smoked salmon napoleon with caviar. Desserts like the signature tower of chocolate—brownie, mousse, and meringue—are edible sculptures. The regional American wine list is superb. *4 World Financial Center, tel. 212/786–1500. Reservations required. Jacket and tie required. AE, D, DC, MC, V. No lunch Sat.*

$$ *Seafood* **Gianni's.** This is the most serious and attractive restaurant near South Street Seaport, an area not noted for gastronomic excellence. Ten pastas, varied antipasto, and garlic bread with Gorgonzola give Italian overtones to the eclectic American menu. Try the roasted lobster with onion-mashed potatoes and chive butter. *15 Fulton St., tel. 212/608–7300. Reservations advised. Dress: casual. AE, DC, MC, V.*

## SoHo and TriBeCa

$$$$ *American-Contemporary* ★ **Chanterelle.** Soft peach walls, luxuriously spaced tables, and flawless service set the stage for David Waltuck's masterpieces, all original, carefully prepared, and beautifully presented, such as the signature seafood sausage, a delicate asparagus flan, and crispy bass with sage. Don't miss such exceptional desserts as chocolate mille-feuille and fruit soup with coconut sorbet. The cheese selection is remarkable. Trust your sommelier to find value in the outstanding wine list. Dinner is prix fixe. In TriBeCa. *2 Harrison St. near Hudson, tel. 212/966–6960. Reservations required. Dress: casual but smart. AE, MC, DC, V. Closed Sun.–Mon.*

$$$ *French* **Montrachet.** Chef Deborah Ponzek's cuisine at this TriBeCa leader, owned by TriBeCa Grill's Drew Nieporent, is at once unpretentious and distinguished by great finesse, as in the outstanding pasta in lobster-truffle cream sauce with foie gras and wild mushrooms, and saddle of rabbit with Swiss chard and turnips. The wine list complements the cuisine beautifully. *239 W. Broadway, between Walker and White,*

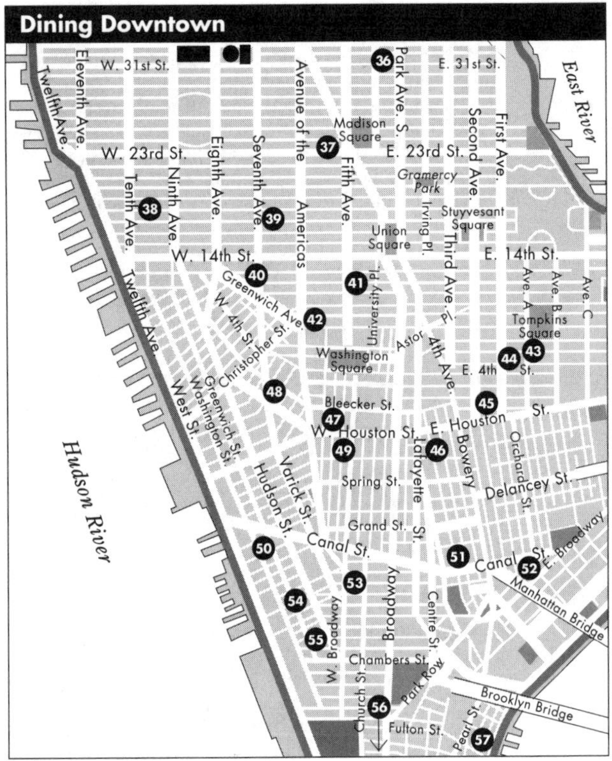


An American Place, **36**
Arturo's, **47**
Ballato's, **46**
Boca Chica, **45**
Bondini, **42**
Capsuto Frères, **50**
Chanterelle, **54**
Duane Park Café, **55**
Dusit Thai, **48**
Follonico, **37**
Gianni's, **57**
Gotham Bar & Grill, **41**
Hudson River Club, **56**
Jean Claude, **49**
La Luncheonette, **38**
Le Madri, **39**
Montrachet, **53**
98 Mott Street, **51**
Pisces, **43**
Takahachi, **44**
Tea and Sympathy, **40**
Triple Eight Palace, **52**

*tel. 212/219–2777. Reservations a must. Dress: casual. AE. Closed Sun.; no lunch Mon.–Thurs. or Sat.*

$$ *American-Contemporary* ★ **Duane Park Café.** This TriBeCa find with a Japanese chef can spoil you with its excellent service, its serious but fairly priced wines, and its eclectic international menu. The design is warm and original, with dark columns and peach walls. *157 Duane St., between W. Broadway and Hudson, tel. 212/732–5555. Reservations required. Dress: casual. AE, D, DC, MC, V. Closed Sat. lunch, Sun.*

*French* **Capsouto Frères.** With its top-notch service, classical music, and reasonable prices, this romantic spot in an 1891 TriBeCa landmark is a winner. Chef Charles Tutino prepares classics with a solid, contemporary touch. Dessert soufflés around town pale against the light, delicious versions here. The carte du vin is sound and tolerably priced. Weekend brunch. *451 Washington St. near Watts, tel. 212/966–4900. Reservations required. Dress: casual. AE, DC, MC, V. No lunch Mon.*

$ *Italian* **Ballato's.** Garlic, red sauce, and soul. This SoHo old-timer can dish up a first-rate veal chop along with winners such as broccoli rabe with sausage, crisp chicken sautéed with olive oil and garlic, and pasta with sardines, pine nuts, and raisins. If you've never tasted tripe, Ballato's version, in a superb marinara sauce, will convert you. Wines are well priced, and most entrées are bargains. *55 E. Houston St., between Mott and Mulberry, tel. 212/274–8881. Reservations advised. Dress: casual. AE, DC, MC, V.*

## Chinatown, Little Italy, and the East Village and Lower East Side

$–$$ *Cantonese* **98 Mott Street.** Like many of New York's Hong Kong–style Chinese restaurants, this one is a virtual palace, with its red and gold accents and attentive waiters in spiffy uniforms. It offers not only low prices but also exciting food. Try the minced scallops in the shell with mushrooms, and the hard-shell crab with chili peppers (first deep fried, then baked in salt). *98 Mott St., between Canal and Hester, tel. 212/*

*226–6603. Reservations only for 4 or more. Dress: casual. AE, MC, V (at dinner only).*

**Triple Eight Palace.** This quintessential Hong Kong–style emporium is wild and wonderful—loud, jam-packed with Chinese families (and lots of babies). It's also one of the pleasantest spots for dim sum. In the evening, you can order excellent seafood, Cantonese specialties, and noodle dishes. To communicate, it helps to bring a Chinese friend. *78 E. Broadway, between Division and Market, tel. 212/941–8886. Reservations only for 6 or more. Dress: casual. AE, DC, MC, V.*

$ *Japanese* ★

**Takahachi.** The best small Japanese restaurant in Manhattan, it's neat and amazingly inexpensive, offering such unusual dishes as fried shiitake filled with ground salmon, chopped tuna sashimi with scallions, seared tuna with black pepper and mustard sauce, and grilled chicken stuffed with plum paste and siso leaf. There's also a good early bird special, served until 7 PM. Wine and beer only. *85 Ave. A, between 5th and 6th, tel. 212/505–6524. No reservations. Dress: casual. AE, MC, V. No lunch.*

*Latin American* ★

**Boca Chica.** This raffish East Villager, hot as a firecracker, has live music, dancing, and assertively seasoned food from several Latin American nations at give-away prices. Check out the soupy Puerto Rican chicken-rice stew known as *asopao*, Cuban sandwiches, Bolivian sweet corn topped with chicken, and the nurturing rice pudding. Try a potent *caipirinha* (lime juice and Brazilian rum). Don't trip over the boa constrictor by the bar. *13 1st Ave. near 1st St., tel. 212/473–0108. No reservations. Dress: casual. AE, DC, MC, V. No lunch Mon.–Sat.*

*Seafood*

**Pisces.** At this striking restaurant, where tables near the open windows seem to spill out into Alphabet City, $15 buys an outstanding three-course dinner. Such sophisticated dishes as smoked salmon terrine with adobo sauce and grilled tuna are incongruous to the East Village scene, but after a delicious dessert it doesn't seem to matter. The wine list is well-chosen and sensibly priced. Brunch is served on weekends. *96 Ave. A at 6th, tel. 212/260–6660. Reserva-*

*tions advised. Dress: casual. AE, MC, V. No lunch weekdays.*

## Greenwich Village

$$$ *American-Contemporary* ★ **Gotham Bar & Grill.** Can success spoil this innovator? Probably not, since management keeps careful watch over the service (generally excellent) and the kitchen (always inventive). Try the sublime pasta filled with caponata and goat cheese, in an intense chicken stock heady with olive oil. The wine list is intelligent, and the lofty, multilevel space was the prototype of the new-style New York restaurant. *12 E. 12th St., tel. 212/620–4020. Reservations advised. Dress: casual. AE, DC, MC, V. No lunch weekends.*

$$ *Italian* **Bondini.** In this multilevel Victorian dining room modest prices belie the refined service and earnest, contemporary kitchen, which shows its stuff in the dill-perfumed codfish soup, asparagus risotto, mustard-sauced veal fillet with apples and mushrooms, and the grand poached pears, served with Kahlua-spiked cream. *62 W. 9th St., between 5th and 6th, tel. 212/777–0670. Reservations advised. Dress: casual. AE, DC, MC, V.*

*French* ★ **Jean Claude.** This bistro from Bouley's former maître d' reflects its owner's eccentric charm and joie de vivre. However, your check buys not only lots of fun but also some of the best bourgeois cooking in town, such as the sautéed tripe on white bean salad and the homemade fettuccine with squid, sun-dried tomatoes, and basil. Note that the phone number is unlisted. *137 Sullivan St., between Houston and Prince, tel. 212/475–9232. No reservations. Dress: casual. No credit cards. No lunch.*

$ *Pizza* ★ **Arturo's.** Guidebooks don't list this brick-walled Village landmark, but the body-to-body crowds teetering on the wobbly wooden chairs suggest good things. The pizza is terrific, cooked in a coal-fired oven; if you want the works, order the Fiesta combo. Basic pastas as well as seafood, veal, and chicken concoctions with mozzarella and lots of tomato sauce come at giveaway prices. *106 W. Houston St., off Thompson, tel. 212/677–3820. No reservations. Dress: casual. AE, MC, V.*

*Tea* **Tea and Sympathy.** This minuscule restaurant offers a terrific English tea and other exports of the United Kingdom. There is a chalkboard menu, and very proper dishes such as Scotch eggs, shepherd's pie, bangers and mash, and scones with clotted cream and jam are served. Desserts are bully, too: trifle and sweet treacle cake, to name but two. On weekends, there's a full English breakfast. *108 Greenwich Ave., between 12th and 13th, tel. 212/807–8329. No reservations. Dress: casual. No credit cards. BYOB.*

*Thai* **Dusit Thai.** Seasoning is forceful here but not unfriendly, and the menu offers many dishes rarely served outside Asia. There are marvelous steamed dumplings with chicken, vegetables, and ground peanuts; deep-fried softshell crabs; whole fish topped with mango, onions, garlic, chile, and lime; and a complex shrimp and chicken curry with lotus seed and coconut milk. *256 Bleecker St., between 6th and 7th, tel. 212/627–9310. Reservations unnecessary. Dress: casual. AE, DC, MC, V. No lunch Sun.*

## Gramercy Park, Murray Hill, Chelsea, and the Flatiron District

$$$ *American-Contemporary* ★ **An American Place.** One of the country's finest regional American restaurants where the menu ranges from adobo-style barbecued duck cake in cornmeal pancakes to homemade peanut butter ice cream sandwiches. There's an excellent all-American wine list. *2 Park Ave., tel. 212/684–2122. Reservations advised. Dress: casual but neat. AE, MC, V. Closed Sat. lunch, Sun.*

*Italian* ★ **Le Madri.** In this Chelsea restaurant, one of Manhattan's top Italians, the menu is at once robust and homey, with dishes such as grilled calamari with fava beans and radicchio, and tagliolini with shrimp, asparagus, and diced tomato. The top-flight service and engaging Tuscan-style space with vaulted ceiling and wood-burning pizza oven add appeal. *168 W. 18th St., tel. 212/727–8022. Reservations advised. Jacket advised. AE, DC, MC, V.*

$$ *Italian* ★ **Follonico.** You'll like the vintage wainscoting, muted colors, and open brick oven, but most of all you will like the food: Tuscan bread salad,

wood-oven–roasted lamb, baby octopus under a net of black pasta. Blueberry granita and caramel semifreddo stand out among the desserts. *6 W. 24th St., tel. 212/691–6359. Reservations required. Dress: casual. AE, DC, MC, V. Closed Sat. lunch, Sun.*

$ *French*

**La Lunchonette.** With its lipstick-red walls, exposed bricks, lace curtains, and long bar, this boîte has a casual bistro charm and an outstanding menu including excellent cassoulet and couscous, and such hard-to-come-by dishes as veal sweetbreads vinaigrette, calves' brains in black butter with capers, and rabbit stew. *130 10th Ave. at 18th, tel. 212/675–0342. Reservations advised. Dress: casual. AE, DC, MC, V. No lunch Sat.–Sun.*

## Midtown

$$$$ *American-Contemporary*

**The "21" Club.** Inside this four-story brownstone landmark the dining room, with banquettes and a ceiling hung with toys, offers traditional American and continental classics, such as the signature "21" burger and chicken hash, and barely cooked scallops encased in a crackling sesame seed crust and garnished with a single potato chip bearing fresh Sevruga caviar. They also boast one of the world's great cellars (with some 50,000 bottles). *21 W. 52nd St., tel. 212/582–7200. Reservations required. Jacket and tie required. AE, DC, MC, V. Closed Sat. lunch, Sun.*

*Japanese*

**Seryna.** This lovely restaurant vividly evokes Tokyo with its dignified air, comfortable seating, and understated colors. Although the sushi is superbly fresh, the specialty is steak Ishiyaki, cooked tableside on a smoldering rock. Cocktails are served in small carafes that come buried in crushed ice. Service is superb. *11 E. 53rd St., tel. 212/980–9393. Reservations advised. Dress: casual. AE, DC, MC, V. Closed Sat. lunch, Sun.*

$$$ *American-Contemporary* ★

**March.** This singular restaurant is supremely, elegantly understated. Service is polished and inconspicuous, and the cuisine is at once restrained and inspired, with such dishes as the sushi-centered tuna tart and tartare, served with roast vegetables, and the impeccable At-

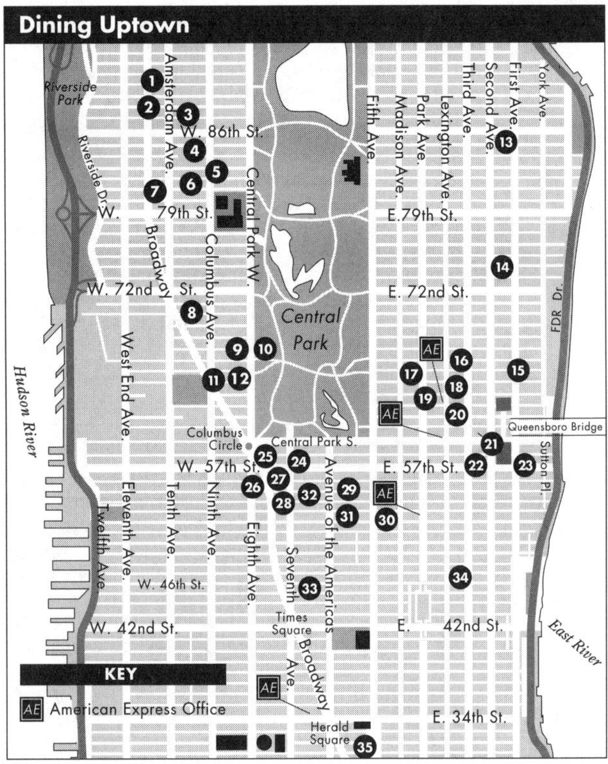


Amsterdam's, **7**
Arizona 206, **21**
Aquavit, **28**
Ben Benson's, **32**
Café Botanica, **24**
Café Crocodile, **14**
Café des Artistes, **9**
Carmine's, **1**
Carnegie Deli, **29**
Chiam, **33**
Dawat, **22**
Dish, **6**
Dock's, **2**
Fujiyama Mama, **5**
Island Spice, **34**
Jack's Firehouse, **4**
JoJo, **18**
Hatsuhana, **33, 35**
JoJo, **18**
L'Auberge, **15**
Le Cirque, **17**
March, **23**
Matthew's, **20**
New York Kom Tang Soot Bul House, **35**
Park Avenue Café, **19**
Picholine, **12**
The Pie, **13**
Popover Café, **3**
San Domenico, **25**
Seryna, **30**
Shun Lee West, **11**
Sign of the Dove, **16**
Symphony Café, **26**
Tavern on the Green, **10**
Trattoria dell'Arte, **27**
The "21" Club, **31**
Ying, **8**

lantic salmon with Middle Eastern spices. The wine list is elite. *405 E. 58th St., tel. 212/838–9393. Reservations required. Jacket advised. AE, DC, MC, V. No lunch; closed Sun.*

*Scandinavian* ★ **Aquavit.** The striking downstairs room in the late Nelson Rockefeller's town house, with its atrium and waterfall, *is* Aquavit. Here you'll find such contemporary Swedish fare as his buckwheat blini with crème fraîche and caviar, roast squab with lemon-braised endive, and desserts such as apple sorbet and chocolate cake with caramelized pear. *13 W. 54th St., tel. 212/307–7311. Reservations required downstairs. Jacket and tie required. AE, DC, MC, V. Closed Sat. lunch, Sun.*

$$ *Chinese* ★ **Chiam.** The setting is stylish, the wine list extraordinary for a Chinese restaurant. Seafood is good; the more interesting dishes, chicken and Chinese sausage steamed in a lotus leaf, for example, are often not on the menu, so solicit your captain's advice. *160 E. 48th St., tel. 212/371–2323. Reservations advised. Dress: casual but neat. AE, DC, MC, V.*

*Indian* **Dāwat.** This classy, understated, spot has flattering lighting, smooth service, and a menu full of consultant Madhur Jaffrey's subtle cuisine: shrimp in mustard seeds with curry leaves, lamb with white turnips, and black-eyed peas and corn. Dāwat demonstrates the charms of Indian sweets; try the pudding-like carrot halva, and *kulfi*, a delicate frozen yogurt. *210 E. 58th St., tel. 212/355–7555. Reservations advised. Dress: casual. AE, DC, MC, V. No lunch Sun.*

$ *Korean* **New York Kom Tang Soot Bul House.** It's the best Korean restaurant on a street jammed with them, and dinner is a show. So come ready for charades (little English is spoken); wear clothes you don't mind getting smoky (from the hibachis in the center of the communal tables); and insist on the attractive second floor. Dinner starts with ten delicious sides, including kim chee, the fiery Korean pickle. *32 W. 32nd St., tel. 212/947–8482. Reservations: difficult if you don't speak Korean. Dress: casual. AE, MC, V.*

## Theater District and Carnegie Hall

$$$–$$$$ *Italian* ★ **San Domenico.** Executive chef Theo Schoenegger executes dishes such as Mediterranean baby cuttlefish with vegetables, soft egg-yolk ravioli with truffle butter, and roast baby goat with authority. The setting is like a private villa, with terra-cotta floors, sumptuous leather chairs, and lots of warm, earthy hues. *240 Central Park S, tel. 212/265–5959. Reservations required. Jacket and tie required; on Sun., casual but neat. AE, DC, MC, V. No lunch weekends.*

$$$ *Steak* **Ben Benson's.** Steaks, chops, and accompaniments are first-rate in this convivial spot with a rather masculine interior and a no-nonsense atmosphere. Witness such contemporary steak house fare as cold lobster cocktail and Maryland crab cakes; steak, chops, and the fabulous prime rib. The wine list is carefully chosen. *123 W. 52nd St., tel. 212/581–8888. Reservations advised. Dress: casual. AE, DC, MC, V. Closed Sat., Sun. lunch.*

$$ *American-Contemporary* ★ **Symphony Café.** At this upscale brasserie near Carnegie Hall, decked with gold records and autographed photographs of songwriters, executive chef Neil Murphy's food is first-rate: Try the homey wood-grilled chicken with chanterelles or delicious pan-roasted cod with lobster home fries. *950 8th Ave. at 56th, tel. 212/397–9595. Reservations accepted. Dress: casual but neat. AE, DC, MC, V.*

*French* **Café Botanica.** At this glorious café, which is as airy as the country with its high ceilings, wicker chairs, Central Park views, and striking Elke Sommer painting, the food is inventive and elegant. Standouts include sautéed foie gras on green lentils, porterhouse with mashed potatoes and chives, and seared salmon with celery root–sorrel coulis. *160 Central Park S, tel. 212/484–5120. Reservations advised. Dress: casual but neat (no jeans). AE, DC, MC, V.*

*Italian* **Trattoria dell'Arte.** This top trattoria still displays the controversial oversize renderings of body parts. But the real draw nowadays is the delicious cuisine, like the linguini with red bean sauce and shiitake mushrooms, and the incredible whole fish with green olives and white wine.

Double veal chops are mammoth, desserts fabulous. Weekends, there's brunch. *900 7th Ave., between 56th and 57th, tel. 212/245–9800. Reservations advised. Dress: casual. AE, DC, MC, V.*

$–$$ *Italian* **Carmine's.** This cavernous family-style eatery, which started on the West Side, soon moved to Broadway. It's a good show. (*See* Upper West Side.) *200 W. 44th St., tel. 212/221-3800. Reservations accepted. Dress: casual. AE.*

$ *Deli* **Carnegie Deli.** Although not what it was, this no-nonsense spot is still midtown's best deli, a species distinguished by crowds, noise, brusque service, and jumbo sandwiches. Try to get the counterman to hand-slice your corned beef or pastrami; the extra juiciness and superior texture warrant the extra charge. *854 7th Ave., between 54th and 55th, tel. 212/757–2245. No reservations. Dress: casual. No credit cards.*

*Jamaican* **Island Spice.** This spotless and altogether delightful spot, with green walls and plastic tablecloths, offers some of New York's best Caribbean fare. The kitchen's gastronomic reggae shows up in such dishes as the zesty jerk pork and chicken barbecue; and the tender, curried goat meat, which you stuff into Indian flatbread—what a terrific sandwich. *402 W. 44th, tel. 212/765–1737. Reservations advised. Dress: casual. AE, DC, MC, V.*

## Upper East Side

$$$$ *French* ★ **Le Cirque.** The rich, the famous, and dentists from Des Moines all want to dine at this palace of international luxury; one comes here not to eat, but for the experience—although the food is of the highest quality. The cuisine includes tuna tartare with a hint of curry, scallops and truffles in pastry, and lobster and rosemary risotto. *58 E. 65th St., tel. 212/794–9292. Reservations required. Jacket and tie required. AE, DC, MC, V. Closed Sun.*

$$$ *American-Contemporary* **Park Avenue Café.** American folk art, antique toys, and sheafs of dried wheat decorate this unpretentious dazzler. Favorite dishes are the delicate flan of prosciutto, peppers, and foie gras that comes in an egg shell held by a porcelain

rabbit, and the seared salmon with ginger resting on an inverted vase. *100 E. 63rd St., tel. 212/644–1900. Reservations advised. Dress: casual. AE, DC, MC, V. Closed Sat., lunch.*

**Sign of the Dove.** Skylights, stunning floral arrangements, well-spaced tables, brick arches, and piano music distinguish the dining rooms here, some of the prettiest in town. Don't miss the titillating Thai-spiced crab chowder, the mouthwatering Moroccan-inspired lamb bastilla, or the pan-seared tuna in green curry broth. *1110 3rd Ave. at 65th, tel. 212/861–8080. Reservations required. Jacket and tie advised. AE, DC, MC, V. No lunch Mon.*

*Southwestern*
★

**Arizona 206.** Stucco walls and blanched wood create a desert look here and the less expensive adjacent Arizona Café. But no Mojave truck stop serves dishes like executive chef David Walzog's lively pan-seared scallops, presented here with roasted garlic and pumpkin-seed pesto, or the spicy grilled rabbit in cilantro oil. *206 E. 60th St., tel. 212/838–0440. Dress: casual but neat. AE, DC, MC, V. No Sun. lunch.*

**$$**
*American-Contemporary*

**Matthew's.** This hot café is airy and attractive with its white shutters, ceiling fans, jumbo potted plants, and warm colors. Young chef Matthew Kenny has an eclectic contemporary style. You'll find tuna tartare (more coarsely chopped here than in most new American restaurants), served with a Mediterranean green olive tapenade. *1030 3rd Ave. at 61st, tel. 212/838–4343. Reservations advised. Dress: casual. AE, DC, MC, V.*

**Jo Jo.** At this chic spot most of chef Jean-Georges Vongerichten's creations are impressive, including such dishes as sweetbreads with chestnut-truffle vinaigrette, scallops with chopped raw beets and parsley juice, pork cheeks and black bean salad, and sautéed bass, gutsy in its salsify broth. *160 E. 64th St., tel. 212/223–5656. Reservations required. Dress: casual but neat. AE, MC, V. Closed Sat. lunch, Sun.*

*Mediterranean*

**Café Crocodile.** A meal in this diminutive charmer is like eating in a private home. Andrée Abramoff cooks in the classic European style, but strong Mediterranean and Middle Eastern influences show up in the smoky baba ghannoush (eggplant purée) and hummus (chickpea purée), the homey couscous, and the whole red snapper. *354 E. 74th St., tel. 212/249–6619. Reservations required. Dress: casual but neat. AE.*

$ *Middle Eastern* ★ **L'Auberge.** With its flattering lighting and elegant decor, L'Auberge recalls Paris more than Beirut. You'll know it's Lebanese when you dig into the delicious hummus, smoky baba ghannoush, and *kibbee* (ground lamb). Go with a group and sample the assorted *mezze* (appetizers). The $6.95 all-you-can-eat weekday lunch buffet is a steal. *1191 1st Ave., between 64th and 65th, tel. 212/288–8791. Reservations accepted. Dress: casual. AE, DC, MC, V.*

*Russian* **The Pie.** This pint-size slice of what used to be called the Soviet Union, transplanted to a Yorkville storefront, specializes in Russian pies, made from crepes arranged in a casserole and bursting with your choice of filling. Blini with herring, salmon caviar, and smoked salmon are divine appetizers. Soups are honest and satisfying. Entrées include filet mignon pie and chicken Rasputin. *340 E. 86th St., tel. 212/517–8717. Reservations advised. Dress: casual. AE.*

## Lincoln Center

$$$ *American-Contemporary* **Tavern on the Green.** The reception is perfunctory, the service inept (if usually polite), and the food still hit or miss (although improved thanks to the direction of Marc Poidevin). Still, Warner LeRoy's lavish restaurant is a visual fantasy, and careful selection can yield a satisfying meal. There's also jazz, dancing, and cabaret. *In Central Park at 67th St., tel. 212/873–3200. Reservations advised. Jacket advised. AE, DC, MC, V.*

*French* **Café des Artistes.** Writer-restaurant consultant George Lang's masterpiece is snug and beautiful with its polished oak woodwork and rosy Howard Chandler Christy murals. The cuisine of chef Thomas Ferlesch is as refined as the setting and it would be hard to find a better *pot au feu*, a French variation on pot roast. *1 W. 67th St., tel. 212/877–3500. Reservations required. Jacket and tie required at dinner. AE, DC, MC, V.*

$$ *Chinese* ★ **Shun Lee West.** It's a dramatically lighted study in black, accented by white dragons and monkeys. Try Peking duck, sweetbreads with hot peppers and scallions, or rack of lamb Szechuan-style. *43 W. 65th St., tel. 212/595–8895. Reservations advised. Jacket requested. AE, DC, MC, V.*

*Mediterranean* ★ **Picholine.** Dried flowers, plaid fabrics, and rough stucco create a rustic look here. Homemade breads are impressive, as are the Mediterranean spreads with just-out-of-the-oven flat bread. Don't miss the luscious duck risotto with wild mushrooms, pumpkin, and white truffle oil. *35 W. 64th St., tel. 212/724–8585. Reservations advised. Dress: casual. AE, DC, MC, V. Closed Mon. lunch, Sun.*

$ *Chinese* **Ying.** Charming, energetic Tina Ying runs an attractive Cantonese-Szechuan restaurant with inviting wicker chairs, live piano music, and excellent service. Vietnamese chicken rolls are uncommonly crisp and orange chicken is perfect. *117 W. 70th St., tel. 212/724–2031. Reservations accepted. Dress: casual. AE, MC, V.*

## Upper West Side

$$ *American-Casual* **Popover Café.** This vintage West Side tea room-cum-restaurant full of teddy bears is home to some superb popovers, and there are also terrific soups, plus sandwiches with names like Mad Russian. *551 Amsterdam Ave., between 86th and 87th, tel. 212/595–8555. Reservations advised. Dress: casual. AE, MC, V.*

*Japanese* **Fujiyama Mama.** White-slipcovered side chairs line up like statues in the vitrine of this creative restaurant with a high-tech design. Dishes have names like Poseidon Adventure and Bermuda Triangle. But the food is serious, inventive, and invariably first-rate. *467 Columbus Ave., between 82nd and 83rd, tel. 212/769–1144. Reservations advised. Dress: casual. AE. Dinner only.*

*Seafood* **Dock's.** The space is small, a slender storefront with lots of black and tan tiles, and the crowd is mainly casual neighborhood types. The menu is dominated by fresh seafood, and their crab cakes are the best in town. *2427 Broadway near*

*90th, tel. 212/724–5588. Dress: casual. Reservations advised. AE, DC, MC, V. No lunch Sat.*

*Italian* ★ **Carmine's.** Dark woodwork and old-fashioned black-and-white tiles make this hotspot look like an old-timer. Kick off a meal with homemade mozzarella-tomato salad or garlicky spedini; move on to the pastas, perhaps rigatoni in a rollicking broccoli, sausage, and white bean sauce. Wines are inexpensive. *2450 Broadway, between 90th and 91st, tel. 212/362–2200. Reservations only for 6 or more. Dress: casual. AE. Dinner only.*

$ *American-Casual* **Amsterdam's.** Tables under the checkered cloths in this unpretentious bistro often need a matchbook, chairs are none too comfortable, and the noise challenges conversation. But the food is reliable and tasty, and there's a different chicken special every day. *428 Amsterdam Ave., between 80th and 81st, tel. 212/874–1377. Reservations not necessary. Dress: casual. AE, MC, V. No lunch Mon.*

**Jack's Firehouse.** There's a reason this find calls itself a firehouse: The sauce they use gives the plain chicken enough kick to get you to Jamaica without an airplane, and the pizza topped with that chicken is not much milder. Still, you can get other varieties, too, and the crust is high, crisp, and delicious. You'll also find good Buffalo wings, chili, and a tasty green salad with sun-dried tomatoes and grilled chicken strips. Or you can try the so-called sexy fries, with cheese dipping sauce, or go for a burger (mild, medium, or inferno). Check out the micro-brewery beers and the brownies. Open until 4 AM. *522 Columbus Ave., between 85th and 86th, tel. 212/787–3473. No reservations. Dress: casual. AE, MC, V.*

*American-Contemporary* **Dish.** Here's the concept: Cook healthy food, cook it well, and serve large portions in huge dishes. Start with a house salad, then have the half rotisserie chicken or the rosemary version on wild rice with vegetables. Or try the spicy pepper steak, served with sautéed peppers and onions. The fat-free, sugar-free cobbler and white chocolate mousse–filled cannoli steal the sweets show. There's Sunday brunch and a wine list that starts at $12. With its rough wood on walls and floors, and its angular, contemporary design, Dish is very pleasant. *100 W. 82nd St., tel. 212/724–8700. Reservations advised. Dress: casual. AE, DC, MC, V. No lunch.*

# 5 Lodging

*By Jane Hershey*

*Updated by Kate Sekules*

If any single element of your trip to New York City is going to cost you a lot of money, it'll be your hotel bill. European cities may offer plenty of low-priced lodgings, but New York tends not to. Real estate is at a premium here, and labor costs are high, so hoteliers start out with a lot of expenses to cover. And there are enough well-heeled visitors to support competition at the premium end of the spectrum, which is where the profits are. Considering the healthy occupancy rate, market forces are not likely to drive current prices down. Fleabags and flophouses aside, there's precious little here for under $100 a night. Furthermore, the city has the country's highest tax rate on hotel rooms: an average of 21¼%. We have noted a few budget properties, but even our "Inexpensive" category includes hotels that run as high as $135 for one night's stay in a double.

Once you've accepted that you must pay the going price, though, you'll have plenty of choices. In general, Manhattan hotels don't measure up to those in other U.S. cities in terms of room size, parking, or outside landscaping. But, this being a sophisticated city, New York hotels usually compensate with fastidious service, sprucely maintained properties, and restaurants that hold their own in a city of knowledgeable diners.

Basic rules of decorum and dress are observed at the better hotels. With few exceptions, jackets (and frequently ties) are required in formal dining and bar areas after 5 or 6 PM. Bare feet or beach sandals are not allowed, and an overall sloppy appearance won't encourage good service.

*Note:* Even the most exclusive hotels have security gaps. Be discreet with valuables everywhere, and stay alert in public areas.

Within each price category, our listings are organized by location. Exact prices could be misleading: Properties change their so-called "rack rates" seasonally, and most hotels offer weekend packages that include such tempting extras as complimentary meals, drinks, or tickets to events. Your travel agent may have brochures about such packages; also look for advertisements in travel magazines or the Sunday travel sections of major newspapers such as the *New*

*York Times*, the *Washington Post*, or the *Los Angeles Times*.

Highly recommended lodgings are indicated by a star ★.

| Category | Cost* |
|---|---|
| $$$$ | over $260 |
| $$$ | $190–$260 |
| $$ | $135–$190 |
| $ | under $135 |

**All prices are for a standard double room, excluding 21¼% city and state taxes.*

Unless otherwise noted in the individual descriptions, all the hotels listed have the following features and services: private baths, central heating, air-conditioning, private telephones, on-premises dining, valet and room service (though not necessarily 24-hour or short-notice), TV (including cable and pay-per-view films), and a routine concierge staff.

New York City has finally allowed liquor minibars to be installed in rooms. Most hotels have added this much-anticipated amenity—at least in their more expensive units.

Pools are a rarity, but most properties have fitness centers; we note only those that are on the premises, but other hotels usually have arrangements for guests at nearby facilities. Some hotels also make nominal charges for guests' use of in-house fitness centers.

## $$$$

★ **The Carlyle.** Museum Mile and the tony boutiques of Madison Avenue are on the doorstep of New York's least hysterical grand hotel, where European tradition and Manhattan swank shake hands. The mood is English manor house; larger rooms and suites, many of them decorated by the famous interior designer Mark Hampton, have terraces, pantries, and antique furnishings. Most visitors have heard about the famous Café Carlyle, where performers such as Bobby Short entertain. But the hotel also con-

Algonquin, **23**
Ameritania, **11**
Beekman Tower, **30**
Best Western Seaport Inn, **36**
Broadway American, **1**
Carlyle, **5**
Chatwal Inn, **21**
Dumont Plaza, **32**
Embassy Suites, **18**
Essex House, **10**
Fitzpatrick, **22**
Gorham, **12**
Holiday Inn Crowne Plaza, **16**
Hotel Edison, **7**
Journey's End, **24**
Loew's N.Y. Hotel, **27**
Mayfair Baglioni, **6**
Michelangelo, **15**
Morgan's, **31**
Paramount, **17**
Pierre, **8**
The Plaza, **9**
Quality Inn, **20**
Radisson Empire, **2**
Renaissance, **19**
Royalton, **25**
The San Carlos, **28**
Sheraton, **14**
Sloane House YMCA, **33**
Southgate Tower, **34**
Surrey Hotel, **4**
Vanderbilt YMCA, **29**
Waldorf-Astoria, **26**
Warwick, **13**
Washington Square Hotel, **35**
West Side YMCA, **3**

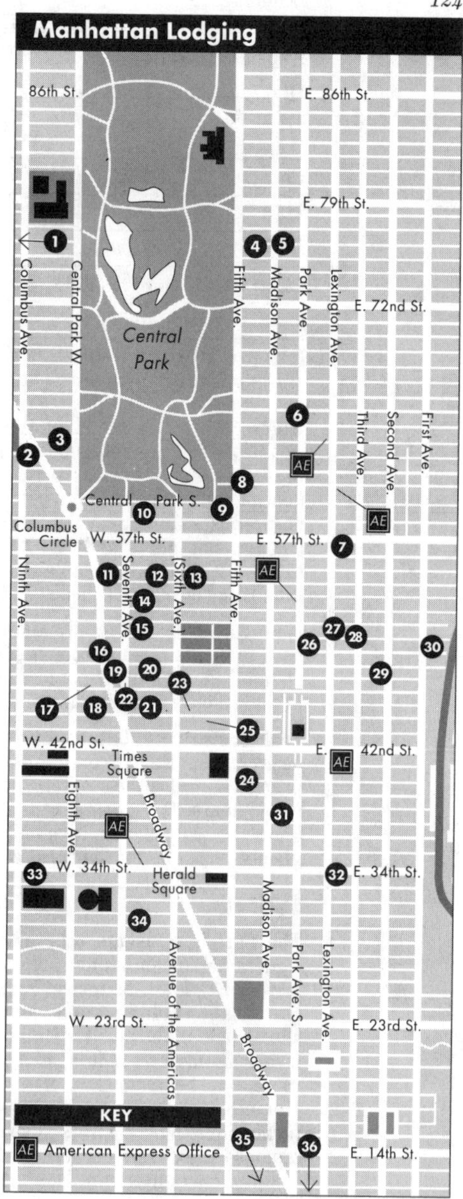

tains the charming Bemelman's Bar, named after Ludwig Bemelman, illustrator of the beloved children's book character Madeline; he created the murals here as well as in the formal Carlyle Restaurant, known for French cuisine and old-fashioned courtly service. There's a jewel of a fitness center that is ultraprivate and luxurious. This is one of the few grand hotels where friendliness and old-school elegance really mix; you don't have to be a famous face to get a smile or good treatment. The concierge and housekeeping service is especially excellent. *35 E. 76th St., 10021, tel. 212/744–1600, fax 212/717–4682. 190 rooms. Facilities: restaurant, café, bar, lounge, VCRs and stereos, fax machines, kitchenettes and pantries in larger units, fitness center, meeting rooms. AE, DC, MC, V.*

★ **Essex House.** The owners, Japan's Nikko Hotels, have done wonders for this stately Central Park South property. The public interiors are an Art Deco masterpiece fit for Fred and Ginger. The talented Christian Delouvrier oversees the cuisine, both in the informal Café Botanica, which faces Central Park and resembles a lush prewar English greenhouse, and in the intimate Les Célébrités. Journey's, the hotel's wood-paneled bar, has a working fireplace. The delights continue upstairs, where guest rooms and baths resemble those in a splendid English country home. The staff is discreet, efficient, and friendly. This is the place to take advantage of weekend rates and book that dreamed-about suite on the park. *160 Central Park S (near 7th Ave.), 10019, tel. 212/247–0300, fax 212/315–1839. 593 rooms. Facilities: 3 restaurants, bar, ballroom, fitness center, meeting rooms, business center. AE, DC, MC, V.*

★ **The Mayfair Baglioni.** General manager Dario Mariotti adds a cheery Italian influence to this low-key, gracious hotel. Locals know it for its traditional tea lounge and its first-rate restaurant, Le Cirque (*see* Chapter 4). Even the smallest of the guest rooms has marble baths and traditional-style, peach-tone decor with up-to-date extras such as dual-line telephones and outlets to accommodate portable computers and fax machines. Service is superefficient; guests are offered umbrellas, room humidifiers, customized pillow selection, and the ingenuity of long-time concierge Bruno Brunelli, who can usually conjure up impossible tickets or reservations. While its overall appearance isn't quite as glitzy as that of some other hotels in this price category, the Mayfair more than makes up for its slightly lived-in feel (which many guests, incidentally, prefer) with friendliness and an always-lively atmosphere. *610 Park Ave., 10021, tel. 212/288–0800 or 800/545–4000, fax 201/737–0538. 150 rooms. Facilities: restaurant, lounge, meeting rooms, unlimited local phone calls. AE, DC, MC, V.*

**The Michelangelo.** The Theater District's only true deluxe hotel, having been through several incarnations, most recently as the Parc 51 and the Grand Bay, seems to have settled happily with the Italian Starhotels company, and is better and friendlier than in the past. A very long, wide, low lobby/lounge caters to Italophiles, with plenty of multihued marble, Vivaldi in the air, and Veronese-esque oil paintings on the walls. Upstairs, the rooms are bigger than they need be, and have either French country decor or a distinctly deco feel (curvy black lacquered or pale oak closets concealing TVs, or fitted bar areas in the larger rooms; much chrome and glass). All have king-size beds, multiline phones, and fine—Italian, of course—marble bathrooms with bidets, TVs, and phones. The staff is helpful, with a concierge who is a cut above the usual found in New York City hotels. *152 W. 51st St., 10019, tel. 212/765–1900 or 800/237–0990, fax 212/581–7618. 178 rooms. Facilities: restaurant, lobby lounge and bar, meeting rooms, fitness center; VCRs, CDs, and fax machines and other business equipment available upon request. AE, DC, MC, V.*

**The Pierre.** Before Canada's Four Seasons hotel group opened its eponymous flagship on 57th Street, the Pierre was its pride and joy, and it remains a high-profile presence. Quite the opposite of the understated style of the Four Seasons, the Pierre's decor owes a lot to the Palace of Versailles, with chandeliers and handmade carpets, murals depicting putti and Corinthian columns in the Rotunda lounge (great for tea), and much muted damask and mahogany in the rooms. It manages not to be ostentatious or stuffy, though, and the staff conveys a sense of fun about working in these posh surroundings. Some $30 million was lavished on renovation a couple of years ago. Bathrooms were upgraded then as well as bedrooms, of which the Boudoir suites, overlooking the Central Park zoo and Wollman Rink, are worth the extra price. This one's a classic whose fans remain faithful. *5th Ave. at 61st St., 10021, tel. 212/838–8000 or 800/332–3442, fax 212/940–8109. 204 rooms. Facilities: restaurant, bar, tearoom, meeting rooms, manned elevators, packing service upon request, hand-laundry service. AE, DC, MC, V.*

**The Plaza.** Occupying the entire southwest corner of Central Park West and 5th Avenue, with its front-yard fountain and unsurpassed location opposite Central Park, the Plaza is probably the most high-profile of all New York hotels. Donald Trump bought it (in 1988), the fictional Eloise ran riot in it (and her "portrait" adorns the fin-de-siècle Palm Court), and film upon film has featured it—from *North by Northwest* in the 1950s and *Breakfast at Tiffany's* and *Barefoot in the Park* in the 1960s, through the 1971 *Plaza Suite*, and the more recent *Sleepless in Seattle*, *Scent of a Woman*, and *Home Alone 2*. Furnishings, though still hotel-like in most units, are of high quality. The color schemes are in burgundy or teal blue; fresh, floral-patterned quilted spreads grace the large beds. Bathrooms, even those not fully redone, have fluffy new towels and toiletries. One real advantage here is the size of guest rooms—only a handful of other classic properties can offer similar spaciousness in nearly all accommodations. *5th Ave. at 59th St., 10019, tel. 212/759–3000 or 800/228–3000, fax 212/546–5324. 807 rooms. Facilities: 2 restaurants, 2 bars, café, art gallery, disabled-accessible rooms, meeting rooms, packing service upon request, large concierge staff. AE, DC, MC, V.*

## $$$

★ **Embassy Suites.** Another welcome addition to the Times Square area, this familiar name's flagship has far more flair than anticipated. The elevated lobby is done up in modern art-deco style; color schemes and furnishings are bold and contemporary. Suites have coffeemakers, small microwave ovens, refrigerators, and even complimentary sodas and snacks. Guest rooms, though hardly elegant, are cheerful and comfortable. Certain suites have been "child-proofed" with such safety features as bumpers placed over sharp edges. All rates include full breakfast and daily cocktails in a private lounge area. There's also a regular restaurant, the Broadway Museum Café, featuring well-priced grills and salads. A complete day-care center with trained staff is just one of many wonderful features for families. The staff seems eager to please, too. Meanwhile, Embassy might improve its street-level security; the block continues to be somewhat unsavory. *1568 Broadway at 47th St., 10036, tel. 212/719–1600 or 800/EMBASSY, fax 212/921–5212. 460 suites. Facilities: restaurant, bar, meeting rooms, day-care center, complimentary use of nearby health club and pool. AE, DC, MC, V.*

**Holiday Inn Crowne Plaza.** The deluxe flagship of the famous commercial hotel chain, a towering roseate stone edifice, was built on the exact site of the original music publishing company of Irving Berlin—he wrote the music for the movie *Holiday Inn,* from which the chain took its name. Public areas with a rose and beige color scheme are softer and more opulent than those of its neighboring competitor, the Marriott Marquis. Upstairs, the decent-size rooms continue the rose color scheme, this time with a touch of teal blue. Guest rooms start at the 16th floor so that everyone gets an eyeful from the panoramic windows. Bathrooms are beyond basic, though the amenities found within could be more lavish. Another minor drawback is the serious lack of closet space, even in the suites. The multi-tiered Samplings bar and restaurant has a terrific view of Broadway. The superior health club includes a shallow lap pool, run by the efficient New York Sports company. *1605 Broadway at 49th St., 10019, tel. 212/977–4000 or 800/HOLIDAY, fax 212/333–7393. 770 rooms. Facilities: 3 restaurants, café, lounge, concierge-level fitness center, pool, ballroom, meeting rooms, business center. AE, DC, MC, V.*

**Renaissance.** The former Ramada Renaissance

was redone to suit the business community, which provides about 70% of its patrons, though for the vacationer, off-season rates start low, and theaterland is on the doorstep. Four Olympian Atlases preside over elevators leading from street level to the third-floor lobby/lounge/reception area, where service is half snotty, half super-friendly, just as decor is half hotel-chain, half deco splendor, with brass and mahogany where chrome and pine suffice elsewhere. Rooms have two-line phones, VCRs, minibars, safes, and bathrooms with deep tubs and a generous selection of toiletries. There's a tiny gym, several boardrooms, secretarial services, and a Mediterranean restaurant called Windows on Broadway, with a great eye-level view of Times Square. Somehow, though, despite the dearth of vinyl and veneer, there's something plasticky about the Renaissance, stemming from its impersonal nature. *2 Times Sq., 10036, tel. 212/765–7676, fax 212/765–1962. 305 rooms. Facilities: restaurant, 2 bars, lounge, business center, meeting rooms, fitness room. AE, D, DC, MC, V.*

**The Royalton.** Ian Schrager and the late Steve Rubell's second Manhattan hotel (Morgan's came first) is a second home to the world's media, music, and fashion biz folk. French designer Philippe Starck transformed spaces of intimidating size into a paradise for poseurs, with vividly colored, geometrically challenged but comfy chairs and couches and lots of catwalk-style gliding areas. The bathrooms are amalgams of raw slate, conical brushed steel, and sculpted water (you have to see them to understand that). Rooms, suffice it to say, are just as glamorously offbeat, some of them oddly shaped and none too big, but all of them perfectly comfortable, especially with the service you get here, which caters to people who feel it's their lot in life to be waited on. The restaurant, 44, is predictably booked solid by New York's style mafia. *44 W. 44th St., 10036, tel. 212/869–4400 or 800/635–9013, fax 212/869–8965. 205 rooms. Facilities: restaurant with bar, lounge, meeting rooms, fitness center, game and library areas, VCRs, stereos. AE, DC, MC, V.*

**The Waldorf-Astoria.** Along with the Plaza (*see $$$$, above*), this Art Deco masterpiece personifies New York at its most lavish and powerful. Hilton, its owner, spent a fortune on refurbishing both public areas and guest rooms a couple of years ago, and the bloom hasn't faded yet, from the original murals and mosaics and elaborate plaster ornamentation to the fine old-wood walls and doors. In the guest rooms, some of which start at the low end of this category, there are new bedspreads, carpets, and other signs of upgrading. Bathrooms throughout are old but beautifully kept up and rather spacious. Of course, in the very private Tower section, everything becomes just that much grander. The chef is French at Peacock Alley, where Waldorf salad first made news; you'll find much more than chopped Macs in mayo nowadays. The Plus One fitness center stresses individual training. The hotel's richly tinted, hushed lobby serves as an interior centerpoint of city life. *301 Park Ave., 10022, tel. 212/355–3000 or 800/HILTONS, fax 212/421–8103. 1,692 rooms. Facilities: 3 restaurants, coffee shop, tearoom, lounge, ballroom, fitness center, meeting rooms. AE, DC, MC, V.*

## $$

**The Algonquin.** While this landmark property's English-drawing-room atmosphere and burnished-wood lobby have been kept mercifully intact, its working parts (the plumbing, for instance) and bedrooms have been renovated. This much-beloved hotel, where the Round Table group of writers and wits once met for lunch, still shelters celebrities, particularly literary types visiting nearby publishing houses or the *New Yorker* magazine offices. Late-night performances go on as usual at the Oak Room. Bathrooms and sleeping quarters retain Victorian-style fixtures and furnishings, only now there are larger, firmer beds, modern TVs, VCRs (upon request), computerized phones, and Caswell-Massey toiletries. *59 W. 44th St., 10036, tel. 212/840–6800 or 800/548–0345, fax 212/944–1419. 165 rooms. Facilities: restaurant, 2 lounges, meeting rooms, complimentary parking on weekends, business center. AE, DC, MC, V.*

**Best Western Seaport Inn.** This thoroughly pleasant, restored 19th-century building is one block from the waterfront, making it convenient for South Street Seaport and lower Manhattan sightseeing, not to mention early morning forays among the ripe aromas of Fulton Street fish market. The decor is somewhere between colonial sea-captain's house and chain hotel (with a video fire crackling in the lobby grate). The reasonably priced rooms feature dark wood, white walls, and floral nylon bedcovers. There's a fine view of Brooklyn Bridge from rooms on the fifth to seventh floors facing Front Street. Ask about weekend rates. *33 Peck Slip, 10038, tel. 212/766–6600 or 800/468–3569, fax 212/766–6615. 65 rooms. AE, DC, MC, V.*

★ **The Fitzpatrick.** This cozy Irish "boutique" hotel is conveniently situated just south of Bloomingdale's and seconds away from anchor bus and subway routes. The first American venture for an established Irish company, it's a real winner in terms of value and charm. Nearly half of the 92 units are true suites that are priced well below the market average, even on weekdays. A small restaurant called Fitzers features Irish seafood in season and a lively bar, which has become popular with locals. The staff is exceptionally friendly and savvy, which may be why celebs such as Gregory Peck and Stephen Rea are checking in. *687 Lexington Ave., 10022, tel. 212/355–0100 or 800/367–7701, fax 212/308–5166. 92 rooms. Facilities: restaurant, bar, small meeting room, fax machines and VCRs available upon request. AE, DC, MC, V.*

**Gorham Hotel.** This small but conveniently located lodging has modern guest rooms and can be recommended to the traveler who wants a location within walking distance of the best of the East and West sides of town. There are pleasant fabrics and carpeting and surprisingly luxurious bathrooms in most units. There is an Italian restaurant downstairs, though one can easily find myriad other dining options nearby. The lobby is bright, and the small staff is informed, if not always overly friendly. *136 W. 55th St., 10019, tel. 212/245–1800 or 800/735–0710, fax 212/245–1800. 120 rooms. Facilities: independent on-premises restaurant, concierge. AE, DC, MC, V.*

**Journey's End.** This Canadian chain's first Manhattan property features no-nonsense, clean, attractive rooms and baths at one fixed price. Most accommodations come with queen-size beds; all have modern TVs and telephones with long cords. Guests can use a small lounge area for complimentary coffee and newspapers. There is an independently owned Italian restaurant on the premises. At night, this part of midtown is somewhat quiet and therefore subject to street crime. However, security at the hotel appears to be superior. Another plus—it's just a few blocks away from the airport bus departure area on Park Avenue near Grand Central Terminal. *3 E. 40th St., 10016, tel. 212/447–1500 or 800/668–4200. 189 rooms. Facilities: lounge, independent on-premises restaurant, business services on request. AE, DC, MC, V.*

**Loews New York Hotel.** Loews's moderate-price New York property has an impersonal style, but most of its regulars—business travelers—don't mind because the hotel generally runs quite well. Rooms, most of them refurbished, are comfortable and well designed. Deluxe units (only slightly higher in price than standard) come with goodies, such as Godiva chocolates and complimentary liquor miniatures. The Lexington Avenue Grill, with striking maroon art-deco carpeting and a wood-tone lobby, has a reliable menu of pastas, burgers, and fish entrées. During low-occupancy periods, guests can actually book rooms here for the upper end of less expensive prices; even suites come down below the $200 range. *Lexington Ave. at 51st St., 10022, tel. 212/752–7000, fax 212/758–6311. 766 rooms. Facilities: restaurant, lounge, meeting rooms, fitness center. AE, DC, MC, V.*

★ **Manhattan Suites East.** Here's a group of good-value properties for the traveler who likes to combine full hotel service with independent pied-à-terre living. These nine midtown hotels have different characters and varying prices, though all have been edging up and most now top the $$ category in busy seasons. The four best are the recently redone **Beekman Tower** (3 Mitchell Pl.), near the United Nations; the **Dumont Plaza** (150 E. 34th St.); the **Surrey Hotel** (20 E. 76th St.), in the neighborhood of Madison Avenue art galleries and designer boutiques; and the **Southgate Tower** (371 7th Ave.), an attractive and secure place to sleep near Madison Square Garden and Penn Station, with the lowest rates of the bunch. Except for the modern style at the Dumont, all have traditional guest-room decor; the Surrey's rooms border on the truly elegant. Most accommodations have pantries, and larger units have dining areas with full-size tables. *Sales office, 505 E. 75th St., 10001, tel. 212/772–2900 or 800/ME-SUITE. AE, DC, MC, V.*

★ **Morgans.** This was the first hotel in nightclub mavens Ian Schrager and the late Steve Rubell's triumphant triumvirate, and you'll find the stunning rooms, created by Andree Putman, are only a little less wacky than at the Starck-designed Royalton (*see* $$$, *above*) and Paramount (*see* $, *below*). From the speckled beige-gray-white walls to the cushions on the windowseat, from the built-in-closet doors to the specially commissioned Mapplethorpe photographs, everything is pretty much in shades that jump between black and white. Exquisite, tiny bathrooms have checkered tile stripes like on the old cabs and snob-value Kiehl's toiletries. If you care deeply about style, can't afford the Royalton, or don't want to be on show, there is no better place to stay in New York. *237 Madison Ave., 10016, tel. 212/686–0300, fax 212/779–8352. 112 rooms. Facilities: breakfast room. AE, DC, MC, V.*

**Radisson Empire Hotel.** A change in ownership transformed this old place into a useful and reliable option. The English country–style lobby is warm and inviting; halls are decorated in soft gray with elegant lamps. Rooms and suites are a bit like small boxes, but nicely furnished; special room features include high-tech electronics, and the small but immaculate baths have heated towel racks. There is a cozy "British" lounge on the second floor that New Yorkers in the know have discovered. Although this hotel's prices have gone up, it's still one of the city's better buys in terms of quality and location, right across the street from Lincoln Center. The neighborhood is loaded with all-hours dining options. *Broadway at 63rd St., 10023, tel. 212/265–7400, 800/221–6509, or 800/223–9868, fax 212/315–0349. 368 rooms. Facilities: voice mail. AE, DC, MC, V.*

**The San Carlos.** This small, residential-style

property offers basic hotel service, clean modern rooms, and a neighborly atmosphere. Larger suites come with kitchenettes, making them a good choice for families. The small wood-paneled lobby is gracious and well lit; women travelers can feel quite secure here. *150 E. 50th St., 10022, tel. 212/755–1800 or 800/722–2012. 140 rooms. Facilities: restaurant. AE, DC, MC, V.*

**The Sheraton New York Hotel & Towers, Sheraton Manhattan.** The Sheraton's multimillion-dollar overhaul of the two buildings for the last Democratic Convention brought vast improvements. Though rooms—even in the superior Tower section located in the Sheraton New York—are on the small side, everything is bright and cheerful. Towers guests have a private lounge and superior amenities, including private check-in and concierge. The New York's restaurant and sports-bar complex, Hudson's, is casual and attractive, as is the Manhattan's Bistro 790, which features surprisingly tasty updated American fare. Non-Tower rooms in the New York and the Manhattan are nearly identical in decor and amenities. The Manhattan has a large renovated pool and a small fitness center, which offers swimming lessons, aquatic exercise, treadmills, and a sun deck. The public spaces of both properties are welcoming, workaday, and busy, busy, busy. Sheraton New York: *811 7th Ave. at 53rd St., 10019, tel. 212/581–1000 or 800/325–3535, fax 212/262–4410. 1,800 rooms.* Sheraton Manhattan: *790 7th Ave. at 51st St., tel. 212/581–3300 or 800/325–3535, fax 212/541–9219. 650 rooms. Combined facilities: 2 restaurants, 2 bars, pool, fitness center, upgraded Tower rooms with private lounge, ballroom, extensive meeting space. AE, DC, MC, V.*

**The Warwick.** Catercorner from the New York Hilton and therefore well placed for theater and points west, this handsome and cozy classic belonging to a Geneva-based chain is still undergoing a major overhaul, with the third through 17th floors complete at press time, and seven more that were scheduled to be finished by summer 1994. Be sure to get one of the new, Regency-style rooms, with hardwood furniture and floral drapes, or you could get stuck in a '70s nightmare of giant bamboo- or autumn leaf-print wallpaper and lurid yellow-tiled bathrooms, with no price difference to lighten the blow. The lobby-lounge is most inviting, with a dark green bar and the huge Tudor murals of the Ciao Europa restaurant on either side of the entrance, lots of armchairs,and marble floors. *65 W. 54th St., tel. 212/247–2700, fax 212/957–8915. 425 rooms. Facilities: restaurant, bar, lounge, meeting rooms. AE, DC, MC, V.*

## $

**Ameritania.** This converted single-room-occupancy hotel is a pleasant choice for the theater goer or business traveler with an eye on the bottom line, and everything from the lobby to the simple rooms is modern and cheerful. Some units have superior baths and amenities. There is a full-service Italian restaurant and small fitness center on the premises. The hotel's proximity to Broadway hits and popular night spots such as the Ritz should keep the clientele on the youthful side. *1701 Broadway, 10019, tel. 212/247–5000, fax 212/247–3316. 250 rooms. Facilities: restaurant, lounge, fitness room. AE, DC, MC, V.*

**Broadway American.** The Upper West Side has become one of New York's hottest neighborhoods. Those wishing to be in its midst should try this small but surprisingly stylish lodging. The least expensive singles have shared baths, though most rooms come with private facilities. Decor is functional modern, with high-tech touches such as TVs with cable. The dominating color scheme is soft gray. The only drawback is that some of this former single-room-occupancy hotel's oddball occupants are living in old-style rooms not yet converted for transient use. *2178 Broadway, 10024, tel. 212/362–1100 or 800/446–4556, fax 212/787–9521. 200 rooms. Facilities: independent on-premises restaurant, vending machines, laundry service, AE, DC, MC, V.*

**Chatwal Inns.** This hotel group features six properties, located mostly in the Broadway-midtown area, that provide clean, attractively designed rooms at relatively unpainful prices. All guests receive a complimentary continental breakfast and discounts to several affiliated restaurants. Some of the larger properties, such as the **Best Western** affiliate (234 W. 48th St.), have on-premises full-service restaurants as well. Rooms, though relatively small throughout all six hotels, are immaculate and have all the basic amenities travelers have come to expect, including bathroom toiletries, modern telephones, and TVs. Since many of the buildings were, until recently, rather dilapidated, don't be put off by the dingy facades of Chatwal properties like **the Quality Inn Midtown** (157 W. 47th St.) or **the Chatwal Inn** (132 W. 45th St.); their interiors are among the chain's nicest. Sant S. Chatwal, owner of Bombay Palace restaurants, is to be applauded for his restoration and pricing efforts. *Tel. 800/826–4667; in Canada: 800/621–4667. Facilities: restaurants, small meeting rooms, lounges, depending on the property. AE, DC, MC, V.*

★ **Hotel Edison.** A popular budget stop for tour groups from here and abroad, this offbeat old hotel has gotten a face-lift. A gruesome murder scene for *The Godfather* was shot in what is now Sophia's restaurant, and the pink-plaster coffee shop has become a hot place to eavesdrop on show-business gossip thanks to such celebrity regulars as Jackie Mason. Guest rooms are brighter and fresher than the dark corridors seem to hint. There's no room service, but this part of the Theater District has so many restaurants and delis that it doesn't matter much. The crowd here is perfectly wholesome, so save money on your room and spend the big bucks on theater tickets. *228 W. 47th St., 10036, tel. 212/840–5000, fax 212/596–6850. 1,000 rooms. Facilities: restaurant, coffee shop, bar. AE, DC, MC, V.*

★ **Paramount.** What used to be the dowdy Century Paramount was completely transformed by the same team that owns the Royalton (*see* **$$$**, *above*) and Morgans (*see* **$$**, *above*) into a cut-rate version of the same, so irresistible it's nearly always full. In the Phillippe Starck lobby, a cliff of concrete and glamorous sweep of staircase lead to a mezzanine gallery area. Rumors that the bedrooms are minute are true. They make up for it with wacky touches, like lights that reproduce the look of dappled sunlight, zebra-striped headboards, and conical steel sinks in the bathrooms—all bearing the Starck stamp—and VCRs as standard issue. There's a Dean & DeLuca takeout off the lobby, and the independently run Brasserie des Theâtres on the other side, plus a fitness center. *235 W. 46th St., 10036, tel. 212/764–5500 or 800/225–7474, fax 212/354–5237. 610 rooms. Facilities: 2 restaurants, privately owned bar, take-out food shop, fitness center, children's playroom, business center, VCRs in rooms. AE, DC, MC, V.*

★ **Vanderbilt YMCA.** Of the various Manhattan Ys offering accommodations, this is the best as far as location and facilities are concerned. Although rooms hold up to four people, they are little more than dormitory-style cells—even with only one or two beds to a room, you may feel crowded. Each room does have a late-model TV, however. There are no private baths; communal showers and toilets are clean. Guests are provided with basics such as towels and soap. Besides the low price, this Y offers membership to its huge health club, which has 2 pools, gym, running track, exercise rooms, and sauna. The Turtle Bay neighborhood is safe, convenient, and interesting (the United Nations is a few short blocks away). Other YMCAs in town include the 561-room **West Side Y** (5 W. 63rd St., 10023, tel. 212/787–4400), which may be hard to get into but is in the desirable Lincoln Center area; and the 1,490-room **Sloane House YMCA** (356 W. 34th St., 10001, tel. 212/760–5860), which is in a gritty and somewhat unsafe neighborhood. *224 E. 47th St., 10017, tel. 212/755–2410, fax 212/752–0210. 430 rooms. Facilities: cafeteria, meeting rooms, self-service laundry, gift shop, luggage storage, 2 pools, fitness center. No credit cards.*

**Washington Square Hotel.** This cozy hotel has a true European feel and style, from the wrought-iron and brass in the small but elegant lobby to the personal attention given by the staff. Rooms and baths are simple but pleasant, not that you'll spend much time in them, with so many shopping, eating, and drinking opportunities on the doorstep. Complimentary continental breakfast is included in the room rate. There's also a good and surpirsingly reasonably priced restaurant, CIII. The manager has strong ties to the local jazz community and can provide tips if you want to catch a set at the nearby Blue Note, or one of the other famous clubs around here. *103 Waverly Pl., 10011, tel.*

*212/777–9515 or 800/222–0418, fax 212/979–8373. 160 rooms. Facilities: independent on-premises restaurant, laundry service. AE, DC, MC, V.*

# 6 The Arts and Nightlife

# The Arts

*By Susan Spano Wells*

*Updated by David Low*

Much has been made of the ballooning cost of tickets, especially for Broadway shows—though major concerts and recitals don't come cheap in New York, either. The top Broadway ticket prices for musicals are $65; the best seats for nonmusicals usually cost $50, although they occasionally hit the $75 mark as well.

On the positive side, tickets for New York City's arts events aren't hard to come by—unless, of course, you're dead set on seeing the season's hottest, sold-out show. Generally, a theater or concert hall's box office is the best place to buy tickets, since in-house ticket sellers make it their business to know about their theaters and shows and don't mind pointing out (on a chart) where you'll be seated.

You can also pull out a credit card and call **Tele-Charge** (tel. 212/239–6200), or **Ticketmaster** (tel. 212/307-4100 for Broadway and Off-Broadway shows, 212/307–7171 for other events) to reserve tickets—newspaper ads generally will specify which you should use for any given event. A surcharge ($2–$5) will be added to the total, and your tickets will be waiting for you at the theater.

Off- and Off-Off-Broadway theaters have their own joint box office called **Ticket Central** (416 W. 42nd St., tel. 212/279–4200). While there are no discounts here, tickets to performances in these theaters are less expensive than Broadway tickets—Ticket Central prices average $10–$35 per person—and they cover an array of events, including legitimate theater, performance art, and dance. Some Off-Broadway plays now allow you to charge tickets through **EZ-TIXZ** (tel. 212/777–7474).

**Discount Tickets**

New York's best-known discount source is the **TKTS booth** in Duffy Square (47th St. and Broadway, tel. 212/768–1818). TKTS sells day-of-performance tickets for Broadway and some Off-Broadway plays at discounts that, depending on a show's popularity, often go as low as half price (plus a $2.50 surcharge per ticket). The names of shows available on that day are posted on boards in front of the booth. If you're interested in a Wednesday or Saturday matinee, go to the booth between 10 and 2, check out what's offered, and then wait in line. For evening performances, the booth is open 3–8; for Sunday matinee and evening performances, noon–8. One caution: TKTS accepts only cash or traveler's checks—no credit cards.

A setup similar to TKTS has arisen in the **Bryant Park Music and Dance Tickets Booth,** located on 42nd Street and 6th Avenue in Bryant Park, just west of the New York Public Library. This booth sells half-price day-of-performance tickets for several music and dance events around the city (and full-price tickets for other concerts as well). It's open Tuesday–Sunday noon–2 and 3–7. Unlike TKTS, the Bryant Park booth has a telephone information line (tel. 212/382–2323). It accepts only cash and traveler's checks.

**Finding Out What's On**

To find out who or what's playing where, your first stop should be the newsstand. The ***New York Times*** isn't a prerequisite for finding out what's going on around town, but it's pretty handy, especially on Friday with its "Weekend" section. On Sunday, the *Times*'s "Arts and Leisure" section features longer "think pieces" on everything from opera to TV—and a lot more ads, plus a full, detailed calendar of cultural events for the upcoming week.

If your tastes are more adventurous, try the weekly paper ***The Village Voice;*** its club listings are unrivaled, its "Choices" section reliable.

In the ***New Yorker*** magazine, "Goings On About Town" heads off each weekly issue with ruthlessly succinct reviews of theater, dance, art, music, film, and nightlife. ***New York*** magazine's "Cue listings" and "Hot Line" section are useful, too. ***Theater Week*** contains up-to-date news on theater happenings all over town. The ***New York Native, Christopher Street,*** and ***Homo-Extra*** cover the gay scene.

## Theater

**Broadway Theater District**

To most people, New York theater means Broadway, that region bounded by 42nd and 53rd streets, between 6th and 9th avenues, where bright, transforming lights shine upon porn theaters and jewel-box playhouses alike.

Some of the old playhouses are as interesting for their history as for their current offerings: the **St. James** (246 W. 44th St.) is where Lauren Bacall served as an usherette in the '40s, and a sleeper of a musical called *Oklahoma!* woke up as a hit; the **Lyceum** (149 W. 45th St.) is New York's oldest still-functioning theater, built in 1903 with a posh apartment on top that now holds the Shubert Archive (open to scholars by appointment only); the **Shubert Theatre** (225 W. 44th St.) is where Barbra Streisand made her 1962 Broadway debut, and the long-run record-breaker, *A Chorus Line,* played for 15 years; and the **Martin Beck Theatre** (302 W. 45th St.), built in 1924 in Byzantine style, is the stage that served up premieres of Eugene O'Neill's *The Iceman Cometh,* Arthur Miller's *The Crucible,* and Tennessee Williams's *Sweet Bird of Youth.* Theater names read like a roll-call of American theater history: **Booth, Ethel Barrymore, Eugene O'Neill, Gershwin, Lunt/Fontanne, Richard Rodgers,** and **Neil Simon,** among others.

Ten years ago it was relatively simple to categorize the New York stage beyond Broadway. It was divided into Off-Broadway and Off-Off-Broadway, depending on a variety of factors that included theatrical contract type, location, and ticket price. Today such distinctions seem strained, as Off-Broadway prices have risen and the quality of some Off-Off-Broadway productions has improved markedly.

Name actors appear in top-flight productions at **Lincoln Center's** two theaters: the **Vivian Beaumont** and the more intimate **Mitzi E. Newhouse** (65th St. and Broadway, tel. for both 212/362–7600), which has scored some startling successes, including John Guare's *Six Degrees of Separation,* and Wendy Wasserstein's *The Sisters Rosensweig.* Downtown at the **Joseph Papp Public Theater** (425 Lafayette St., tel. 212/598–

7150), renamed in 1992 to honor its late founder and long-time guiding genius, producer George C. Wolfe continues the tradition of innovative theater. In the summertime, the Public's Shakespeare Festival raises its sets in Central Park's open-air Delacorte Theater.

One of the major Off-Broadway enclaves is **Theatre Row,** a collection of small houses (100 seats or less)—such as the **John Houseman Theatre** (450 W. 42nd St., tel. 212/967–9077), **Douglas Fairbanks Theatre** (432 W. 42nd St., tel. 212/239–4321), and **Playwrights Horizons** (416 W. 42nd St., tel. 212/279–4200)—on the downtown side of 42nd Street between 9th and 10th avenues. A block east of Theatre Row is the **Westside Theatre** (407 W. 43rd St., tel. 212/307–4100). Another Off-Broadway neighborhood lies in Greenwich Village, around Sheridan Square. Its theaters include the **Actors Playhouse** (100 7th Ave. S., tel. 212/691–6226); **Circle Rep** (99 7th Ave. S, tel. 212/924–7100), a showcase for new playwrights; the **Cherry Lane Theatre** (38 Commerce St., tel. 212/989–2020); the **Lucille Lortel Theatre** (121 Christopher St., tel. 212/924–8782); the **Minetta Lane Theatre** (18 Minetta La., tel. 212/420–8000); the **Perry Street Theatre** (31 Perry St., tel. 212/691–2509); and the **Provincetown Playhouse** (133 MacDougal St., tel. 212/477–5048). Other estimable Off-Broadway theaters are flung across the Manhattan map: the **WPA Theatre** (519 W. 23rd St., tel. 212/206–0523), showcasing new works by American playwrights; the **Promenade Theatre** (Broadway at 76th St., tel. 212/580–1313); and the **Manhattan Theatre Club** (at City Center, 131 W. 55th St., tel. 212/581–1212).

## Music

**Lincoln Center** (W. 62nd St. and Broadway) remains the city's musical nerve center, especially when it comes to the classics. The **New York Philharmonic,** led by musical director Kurt Masur, performs at **Avery Fisher Hall** (tel. 212/875–5030) late September to early June. In summer, the popular **Mostly Mozart** concert series presents an impressive roster of classical performers.

While Lincoln Center is only 30 years old, another famous classical music palace—**Carnegie Hall** (W. 57th St. at 7th Ave., tel. 212/247–7800)—recently celebrated its 100th birthday. This is the place where the great pianist Paderewski was attacked by ebullient crowds (who claimed kisses and locks of his hair) after a performance in 1891; where young Leonard Bernstein, standing in for New York Philharmonic conductor Bruno Walter, made his triumphant debut in 1943; where Jack Benny and Isaac Stern fiddled together; and where the Beatles played one of their first U.S. concerts.

Other prime classical music locales are:

**Merkin Concert Hall** at the Abraham Goodman House (129 W. 67th St., tel. 212/362–8719), almost as prestigious as the concert halls at Lincoln Center.

**Miller Theatre** (Columbia University, Broadway at 116th St., 212/854–7799), featuring a varied program of classical performers, such as the New York Virtuosi Chamber Symphony.

**Kaufman Concert Hall** at the 92nd St. Y (1395 Lexington Ave., tel. 212/996–1100), with the New York Chamber Symphony in residence, plus star recitalists and chamber music groups.

**Bargemusic** at the Fulton Ferry Landing in Brooklyn (tel. 718/624–4061), with chamber music bubbling year-round from an old barge with a fabulous skyline view.

**Brooklyn Academy of Music** (30 Lafayette Ave., tel. 718/636–4100), ever experimenting with new and old musical styles, and still a showcase for the Brooklyn Philharmonic.

## Opera

Recent decades have sharply intensified the public's appreciation for grand opera—partly because of the charismatic personalities of such great singers as Luciano Pavarotti and Jessye Norman, and partly because of the efforts of New York's magnetic **Metropolitan Opera.** A Met premiere draws the rich and famous, the critics, and the connoisseurs. At the Met's elegant Lincoln Center home, with its Marc Chagall murals and weighty Austrian-crystal chandeliers, the supercharged atmosphere gives audiences a sense that something special is going to happen, even before the curtain goes up.

The Metropolitan Opera (tel. 212/362–6000) performs its vaunted repertoire from October to mid-April, and though tickets can cost more than $100, many less expensive seats and standing room are available. Standing room tickets for the week's performance go on sale on Saturday.

The **New York City Opera,** which performs from September through November and in March and April at Lincoln Center's New York State Theater (212/870–5570) continues its tradition of offering a diverse repertoire consisting of adventurous and rarely seen works as well as beloved classic opera and operetta favorites. The Company maintains its ingenious practice of "supertitling"—electronically displaying above the stage, line-by-line English translation of foreign-language operas. Recent seasons have included such old favorites as *Carmen, Madama Butterfly*, and *La Traviata*.

Opera aficionados should also keep track of the **Carnegie Hall** schedule (tel. 212/247–7800) for debuting singers and performances by the Opera Orchestra of New York, which specializes in presenting rarely performed operas in concert form, often with star soloists.

## Dance

The **New York City Ballet,** performs in Lincoln Center's New York State Theater (tel. 212/870–5570). Its winter season runs from mid-November through February—with the beloved annual production of George Balanchine's *The Nutcracker* ushering in the December holiday season—while its spring season lasts from mid-April through June.

Across the plaza at Lincoln Center, the Metropolitan Opera House (tel. 212/362–6000) is home to the **American Ballet Theatre,** renowned for its brilliant renditions of the great 19th-century classics (*Swan Lake, Giselle, The Sleeping Beauty*, and *The Nutcracker*), as well as for the unique scope of its eclectic contemporary repertoire. Its New York season runs from April to June.

When the ABT and NYCB take a break from performing, Lincoln Center acts as impresario for dozens of world-renowned companies, such as the Bolshoi and Royal Danish ballets.

The varied bill at **City Center** (131 W. 55th St., tel. 212/581–7907) often includes touring ballet companies; recently the Matsuyama Ballet from Japan performed there.

A growing international modern dance center is the **Joyce Theater** (175 8th Ave., tel. 212/242–0800), housed in a former Art Deco movie theater. The Joyce is the permanent home of **Feld Ballets/NY,** founded in 1974 by an upstart ABT dancer who went on to become a principal fixture on the dance scene. Other featured companies include the **Garth Fagan Dance** company, the avant-garde **ZeroMoving Company,** and the loony acrobats of **Pilobolus.** At **Symphony Space** (2537 Broadway, tel. 212/864–1414), the bill often features ethnic dance.

Here's a sampling of other, mostly experimental and avant-garde, dance forums:

**Dance Theater Workshop** (219 W. 19th St., tel. 212/691–6500), one of New York's most successful laboratories for new dance.

**Danspace Project** (at St. Mark's-in-the-Bowery Church, 10th St. and 2nd Ave., tel. 212/674–8194), with a series of avant-garde choreography that runs from September through June.

**DIA Center for the Arts** (155 Mercer St., tel. 212/431–9232) hosts a number of performances by interesting local dancers.

**P.S. 122** (150 1st Ave., tel. 212/477–5288), where dance events border on performance art; among others, Meredith Monk occasionally cavorts here.

## Film

The **American Museum of the Moving Image** (35th Ave. at 36th St., Queens, tel. 718/784–0077) is the only U.S. museum devoted to motion pictures, video, and interactive media. Located on the site of the historic Kaufman Astoria Studios, it offers multiple galleries that are a movie buff's paradise, as are its 195-seat Riklis Theatre and 60-seat Warner Communications Screening Room. The museum presents changing exhibits and provocative film programs, including major artist-oriented retrospectives, Hollywood classics, experimental videos, and TV documentaries.

In midtown Manhattan, the **Museum of Television & Radio** (25 W. 52nd St., tel. 212/621–6800 has a gigantic collection of 60,000 radio and TV shows, including everything from *The Dick Van Dyke Show* to *Soap*, *Cheers*, and *Taxi*. The museum's library provides 96 consoles, where you can watch or listen to whatever you wish for up to two hours at a time. The museum presents scheduled theater screenings, gallery exhibits, and series for children.

The Times Square area is still a movie mecca, though action flicks prevail on 42nd Street, and viewers should be warned to sit tight and hold on to their purses.

**Revival Houses**

One of the best places to see old films in Manhattan opened in 1991: the **Walter Reade Theater** at Lincoln Center (70 Lincoln Plaza, Broadway and 65th St., tel. 212/875–5600), operated by the Film Society of Lincoln Center. This comfortable movie house presents several fascinating series that run concurrently, devoted to specific themes or a certain director's body of work; movies for kids are featured Saturday morning. The state-of-the-art auditorium is a little gem with excellent sight lines, and tickets can be purchased at the box office weeks in advance.

Revivals can also be found at:

**American Museum of the Moving Image** (35th Ave. at 36th St., Queens, tel. 718/784–0077), offering American film series, often in historical contexts.

**Film Forum** (209 W. Houston St., tel. 212/727–8110), with three screens showing often quirky series based on movie genres, directors, and other film artists.

**The Museum of Modern Art** (11 W. 53rd St., tel. 212/708–9480), which includes rare classic films in its many series.

**Theatre 80 St. Marks** (80 St. Marks Pl., tel. 212/254–7400), small and shabby but convivial, specializing in double-features from the '30s and '40s.

**Foreign and Independent Films**

**Angelika 57** (225 W. 57th St., tel. 212/586–1900), showing film programs similar to its downtown sister theater (*see below*).

**Angelika Film Center** (W. Houston and Mercer Sts., tel. 212/995–2000), offering several screens devoted to off-beat independent and foreign films, as well as a lively café catering to a youthful crowd.

**Carnegie Hall Cinemas** (887 7th Ave., between 56th and 57th Sts., tel. 212/265–2520), where intriguing new films find long runs.

**Cinema Village 12th Street** (12th St., between 5th Ave. and University Pl., tel. 212/924–3363), offering innovative independent features and occasional animation festivals.

**Eastside Playhouse** (3rd Ave., between 55th and 56th Sts., tel. 212/755–3020), with an emphasis on first-run art films.

**Film Forum** (209 W. Houston St., tel. 212/727–8110) presenting some of the best new independent films and hard-to-see foreign movies.

**The Joseph Papp Public Theater** (425 Lafayette St., tel. 212/598–7171), a reliable forum for experimental and independent film.

**Lincoln Plaza** (Broadway, between 62nd and 63rd Sts., tel. 212/757–2280), six subterranean cinemas playing long-run foreign hits.

**Loews Paris** (58th St., between 5th and 6th Aves., tel. 212/980–5656), a showcase for much-talked-about new American and foreign entries.

**68th Street Playhouse** (3rd Ave. at 68th St., tel. 212/734–0302), with exclusive extended runs of critically acclaimed films.

**Quad Cinema** (13th St., between 5th and 6th Aves., tel. 212/255–8800), with first-run Hollywood, art, and foreign films.

**Village East Cinemas** (2nd Ave. at 12th St., tel. 212/529–6799), presenting cutting-edge independent features alongside mainstream Hollywood productions.

# Nightlife

*By Susan Spano Wells*

*Updated by Andrew Collins*

## Clubs and Entertainment

On Friday, the *New York Times*'s "Weekend" section carries a "Sounds Around Town" column that can give you a picture of what's in the air, as can the *Village Voice,* which probably has more nightclub ads than any other rag in the world. Or stop by Tower Records (Broadway and E. 4th St., tel. 212/505–1500; Broadway and W. 66th St., tel. 212/799–2500), where fliers about coming events and club passes are stacked outside. You may also get good tips from a suitably au courant hotel concierge. Just remember that what's hot and what's not changes almost weekly in this city, so visitors are at a distinct disadvantage. Most clubs will charge a cover of at least $10 a head; some go as high as $20–$50 (nobody said catting around was going to be cheap!). Take cash because many places don't accept plastic.

**Putting on the Ritz**

**The Ballroom** (253 W. 28th St., tel. 212/244–3005). This very hip Chelsea spot has an extensive tapas bar and a nightclub where some of the great chanteuses—including Phoebe Légère and Helen Schneider—rhapsodize, and where Broadway's best moonlight after the shows on their nights off.

**The Carlyle** (35 E. 76th St., tel. 212/744–1600). The hotel's discreetly sophisticated Café Carlyle is where Bobby Short plays when he's in town; otherwise, you might find Eartha Kitt purring by a piano. Bemelmans Bar, with murals by the author of the Madeline books, regularly stars jazz pianist Barbara Carroll.

**Nell's** (246 W. 14th St., tel. 212/675–1567). Back in vogue, Nell Campbell (of *Rocky Horror* fame) reintroduced sophistication to nightlife with her club. The tone in the upstairs jazz salon is Victorian; downstairs is for tête-à-têtes and dancing. The boîte opens at 10 PM and closes at 3 AM (4 AM weekends).

**The Rainbow Room** and **Rainbow and Stars Club** (30 Rockefeller Plaza, tel. 212/632–5000). You can find two kinds of heaven high up on Rockefeller Center's 65th floor. The Rainbow Room serves dinner, and dancing to the strains of a live orchestra takes place on a floor right out of an Astaire-Rogers musical. At the intimate Rainbow and Stars Club, singers such as Maureen McGovern and Rosemary Clooney entertain, backlit by a view of the twinkling lights of the city.

**Jazz Notes**

**Birdland** (2745 Broadway, tel. 212/749–2228). Although way up on the West Side (at 105th St.), this spot is still close to the Village at heart. You'll find lots of up-and-coming groups here.

**The Blue Note** (131 W. 3rd St., tel. 212/475–8592). This club may be the jazz capital of the world. Just an average week could bring Spyro Gyra, the Modern Jazz Quartet, and Joe Hendricks. Expect a steep music charge.

**Bradley's** (70 University Pl., tel. 212/228–6440). With brighter-than-usual lighting and, generally, jazz piano (and sometimes a sax), this is a spot for serious fans of jazz.

**Dan Lynch's Blues Bar** (221 2nd Ave., tel. 212/677–0911). This jazz surprise in the East Village bustles, with jam sessions on Saturday and Sunday afternoons.

**The Knitting Factory** (47 E. Houston St., tel. 212/219–3055). It looks seedy on the outside, but inside there's often fine avant-gardish jazz, anything from a trio to a full orchestra.

**The Village Vanguard** (178 7th Ave. S, tel. 212/255–4037). This old Thelonius Monk haunt, the prototype of the old-world jazz club, lives on in a smoky cellar.

**Rock Around the Clock**

**CBGB & OMFUG** (315 Bowery, tel. 212/982–4052). The full name is "Country Blue Grass Blues & Other Music For Uplifting Gourmandizers," which basically means: rock. American punk rock was born here, in this long black tunnel of a club featuring bands with inventive names: Die Monster Die, the Lunachicks, and Iron Prostate.

**Continental Divide** (25 3rd Ave., tel. 212/529–6924). This knockdown version of CBGB appeals to thrifty college kids on their last nickel.

**The Rock 'n' Roll Café** (149 Bleecker St., tel. 212/677–7630). A week's worth of band names should clue you in: the Maudlins, the Illegitimate Sons of the Blues Brothers, and of course, Kiss My Cobra.

**Wetlands Preserve** (161 Hudson St., tel. 212/966–5244). Billed as a "watering hole for activists," recent acts have included Mountain and Alex Chilton.

**Comic Relief**

**Caroline's Comedy Club** (1626 Broadway, between 49th and 50th Sts., tel. 212/757–4100). This popular club features established names as well as comedians on the edge of stardom.

**Catch a Rising Star** (1487 1st Ave., tel. 212/397–3000). Johnny Carson got his start here, and talent scouts still show up to test the comic current. This place is neither trendy nor cutting edge, but it is reliable.

**Chicago City Limits** (351 E. 74th St., tel. 212/772–8707). This troupe's been doing improvisational comedy for a long time, and it seldom fails to whip its audiences into a laughing frenzy. Chicago City Limits performs in an East Side church and is very strong on audience participation.

**Comedy Cellar** (117 MacDougal St., tel. 212/254–3630). This spot has been running for some years now beneath the Olive Tree Café, with a bill that's a good barometer of who's hot.

**The Improvisation** (433 W. 34th St., tel. 212/279–3446). The Improv, which moved to a bigger home in 1993, is to comedy what the Blue Note is to jazz. Lots of now-famous comedians got their first laughs here, among them Richard Pryor and Robin Williams.

## Bars

**Vintage Classics**

**The Algonquin Hotel Lounge** (59 W. 44th St., tel. 212/840–6800). This is a venerable spot, not only because it was the site of the fabled literary Round Table, but also for its elegant tone.

**Elaine's** (1703 2nd Ave., tel. 212/534–8103). The food's nothing special, and you will be relegated to an inferior table, but go to crane your neck and gawk. Woody Allen's favorite table is by the cappuccino machine. It's best to visit late, when the stars rise in Elaine's firmament.

**King Cole Bar** (at the St. Regis Hotel, 2 E. 55th St., tel. 212/753–4500). The famed Maxwell Parrish mural is a welcome sight at this midtown landmark, happily open again following a thorough and sensitive restoration.

**The Oak Bar** (at the Plaza Hotel, 5th Ave. and 59th St., tel. 212/759–3000). With its plummy, dark-wood furnishings, this old favorite continues to age well. Its great location draws sophisticates, shoppers, tourists in the know, and stars.

**The River Café** (1 Water St., Brooklyn, tel. 718/522–5200). An eminently romantic spot, hidden at the foot of the Brooklyn Bridge, this restaurant offers smashing views of Wall Street and the East River.

**"21" Club** (21 W. 52nd St., tel. 212/582–7200). Famous for its old-time club atmosphere even before it was filmed in *All About Eve*, this isn't exactly a swinging joint, but its conservative environs evoke a sense of connections, power, and prestige. It's tough to get in unless you plan to eat here, too (*see* Chapter 4).

**Drinking Spots Around Town**

*Chelsea and the Village*

**Cedar Tavern** (82 University Pl., tel. 212/243–9355). Here's a very informal, warm spot for a post-double-feature beer.

**Chumley's** (86 Bedford St., tel. 212/675–4449). There's no sign to help you find this place—they took it down during Chumley's speakeasy days—but when you reach the corner of Barrow Street, you're very close. A fireplace warms this relaxed spot where the burgers are hearty, and the kitchen stays open past 10 PM.

**Coffee Shop** (29 Union Sq. W, tel. 212/243–7969). A hip, 23-hour-a-day hangout from Tuesday through Saturday (closed 6–7 AM), the place is fueled by attitude. (Open 20 hours Sunday and Monday; closed 3–7 AM.)

**McSorley's Old Ale House** (15 E. 7th St., tel. 212/473–9148). One of New York's oldest saloons (opened in 1854), this is a must-see for first-timers to Gotham.

**Peter MacManus Café** (152 7th Ave., tel. 212/463–7620). It's known simply as MacManus's to the regulars, who like this bar's unpretentiousness. Among them are lots of actors, fresh from classes in the neighborhood.

**Pete's Tavern** (129 E. 18th St., tel. 212/473–7676). This saloon is famous as the place where O. Henry wrote "The Gift of the Magi" (at the second booth to the right as you come in). These days, it's still crowded with noisy, friendly souls.

**The White Horse Tavern** (567 Hudson St., tel. 212/243–9260). Famous among the literati, this is the place where Dylan Thomas drained his last cup to the dregs. From April through October, there's outdoor café drinking.

*Midtown and the Theater District*

**Barrymore's** (267 W. 45th St., tel. 212/391–8400). This is a pleasantly downscale Theater District spot, with the requisite show posters on the wall. Listen in on the conversations at the bar and you'll hear a few tawdry, true stories of what goes on behind Broadway stage doors.

**Café Un Deux Trois** (123 W. 44th St., tel. 212/354–4148). This old hotel lobby, charmingly converted, is chicly peopled. The bar itself is small, but it's a hot spot before and after the theater.

**Century Café** (132 W. 43rd St., tel. 212/398–1988). An immense vintage neon sign lights up the bar at this trendy, friendly Theater-District bistro where you *won't* find the requisite show posters.

**Halcyon Bar** (at the Rihga Royal Hotel, 151 W. 54th St., tel. 212/307–5000). A big, airy hotel bar, with large and well-spaced tables, it's great for a private chat.

**Hard Rock Café** (221 W. 57th St., tel. 212/459–9320). Formerly embraced by the kids of stars—now, in fact, its clientele seems eternally prepubescent kids accompanied by muttering parents who find it big, crowded, and far too noisy for talk.

**Planet Hollywood** (140 W. 57th St., tel. 212/333–7827). It's touristy, it doesn't take reservations, and waiting lines are long. Still, the place has cachet, an undeniable star quality, and such movie memorabilia as C3PO and Dorothy's red shoes, which make up for the very compact bar.

**Sardi's** (234 W. 44th St., tel. 212/221–8440). "The theater is certainly not what it was," croons a cat in *Cats*—and he could be referring to this venerable spot as well. Still, if you care for the theater, don't leave New York without visiting this establishment.

**The Whiskey** (at the Paramount Hotel, 235 W. 46th St., tel. 212/764–5500). A downstairs bar graces this chic, revamped Times Square hotel that's sleek and hip, and ideal après-theater. Also fun for evening drinks is the mezzanine lounge, pure Philippe Starck-meets-the-'40s. Wear black.

*East Side* **Jim McMullen's** (1341 3rd Ave., tel. 212/861–4700). A young, quintessential Upper East Side watering hole, McMullen's has a large, busy bar decked with bouquets of fresh flowers. Here you'll find lots of Gold Cards, tennis talk, and alumni fund gatherings.

**The Polo Lounge** (at the Westbury Hotel, 15 E. 69th St., tel. 212/439–4835). This place is, in a word, classy; it's frequented by European royalty and Knickerbocker New York.

*West Side* **Dublin House** (225 W. 79th St., tel. 212/874–9528). Above the door glows a small neon harp; inside you'll find lots of very young professionals, Columbia students, and softball teams throwing back two-bit drafts.

**Lucy's Retired Surfer Bar** (503 Columbus Ave., tel. 212/787–3009). One of the many bars to claim to be "Home of the Jello Shot," this southern California–Mex hangout is a hit with young Upper West Siders, who pack themselves into the bar area and sometimes even manage to dance. The decor is playful gulf beach hut.

## Gay Bars

**Men's Bars** **Cleo's 9th Avenue Saloon** (656 9th Ave., tel. 212/307–1503). Near the Theater District, this small, narrow neighborhood bar draws a convivial, laid-back older crowd.

**Crowbar** (339 E. 10th St., tel. 212/420–0670). Gay grungers and NYU students mingle happily at this East Village hot spot. Very big on Wednesday and Friday.

**Stonewall** (53 Christopher St., tel. 212/463–0950). An odd mix of tourists chasing down gay history and down-to-earth locals, the scene is everything but trendy.

**The Works** (428 Columbus Ave., tel. 212/799–7365). Whether it's Thursday's $1 margarita party, or just a regular Upper West Side afternoon, the crowd is usually J. Crew–style or disco hangover.

**Women's Bars** **Crazy Nanny's** (21 7th Ave. S, tel. 212/366–6312). The crowd is wide-ranging—from urban chic to shaved head—and tends toward the young and wild side.

**Henrietta Hudson** (438 Hudson St., tel. 212/243–9879). A little more upscale than Crazy Nanny's. The dance floor here is tiny but well utilized.

**Julie's** (204 E. 58th St., tel. 212/688–1294). Popular with the sophisticated-lady, upper-crust crowd, this brownstone basement has a piano bar.

# Index